Challenges in Securities Markets Regulation:
Investor Protection and Corporate Governance

CHALLENGES IN SECURITIES MARKETS REGULATION: INVESTOR PROTECTION AND CORPORATE GOVERNANCE

Edited by and Introduction by
Pablo Gasós, Ernest Gnan and Morten Balling

Contributions by
Paul Tucker
Michael Haliassos
Theodor Kockelkoren
Juan Carlos Ureta
José Manuel González-Páramo
Lori J. Schock
Colin Mayer
Eddy Wymeersch

A joint publication with the CNMV The Comisión Nacional del Mercado de Valores

SUERF – The European Money and Finance Forum
Madrid & Vienna 2015

SUERF Study 2015/1

 larcier

CIP

Challenges in Securities Markets Regulation: Investor Protection and Corporate Governance

Editors: Pablo Gasós, Ernest Gnan and Morten Balling

Authors: Paul Tucker, Michael Haliassos, Theodor Kockelkoren, Juan Carlos Ureta, José Manuel González-Páramo, Lori J. Schock, Colin Mayer & Eddy Wymeersch

Keywords: Securities markets, design of regulation, disclosure requirements, transparency, stock exchanges, investor protection, financial supervision, prudential regulation, regulatory arbitrage, constrained discretion, risk management, risk committees, financial stability, financial education, financial literacy and capability, financial inclusion, incentive structure, financial advice, conflicts of interest, complexity of financial products, product-based and user-based regulation, borrower protection, advice practices, certification of advisors, quality of prospectuses, rule books, active and passive funds, execution only, investment performance, loan performance, corporate governance, market discipline

JEL-codes: D14, D18, D82, D83, G11, G14, G18, G21, G28, G32, K22.

Vienna: SUERF (SUERF Studies: 2015/1) – March 2015

ISBN: 978-3-902109-76-7

© 2015 SUERF, Madrid & Vienna

TABLE OF CONTENTS

LIST OF AUTHORS

José Manuel GONZÁLEZ-PÁRAMO
Member of the Board of Directors and Chief Officer, Global Economics, Regulation and Public Affairs, BBVA

Michael HALIASSOS
Professor and Chair for Macroeconomics and Finance, Goethe University Frankfurt and Director of the Center for Financial Studies and of SAFE

Theodor KOCKELKOREN
Member of the Executive Board, AfM and Chairman of the OECD Task Force on Financial Consumer Protection

Colin MAYER
Professor of Management Studies Saïd Business School, University of Oxford

Lori J. SCHOCK
Director, Office of Investor Education and Advocacy, US Securities and Exchange Commission (SEC)

Paul TUCKER
Senior Fellow, Harvard University, and former Deputy Governor of the Bank of England

Juan Carlos URETA
President of Renta4 and of Fundación de Estudios Financieros

Eddy WYMEERSCH
Professor University of Gent, ECGI Fellow

1. INTRODUCTION

Pablo Gasós[1], Ernest Gnan[2] & Morten Balling[3]

On November 14th, 2014, SUERF – The European Money and Finance Forum – and CNMV, Comisión Nacional del Mercado de Valores – the Spanish Authority for supervision of securities markets – jointly organized a conference in Madrid: *Challenges in Securities Markets Regulation: Investor Protection and Corporate Governance*. The conference was part of the activities arranged to celebrate the 25th anniversary of the creation of the CNMV. The present SUERF Study includes a selection of papers based on the authors' contributions to the Madrid conference.

In chapter 2, *Paul Tucker*, Senior Fellow, Mossavar-Rahmani Center for Business and Government, Harvard Kennedy School and Harvard Business School, former Deputy Governor of the Bank of England discusses the topic: "Fundamental challenges for securities regulation: a political economy crisis in the making?" The traditional role of securities regulators was to enforce disclosure so that investors had access to all materially relevant information. Regulators also approved, overrode or substituted for the rules of securities exchanges and market bodies, which were essentially self-regulating trade associations. The regulator's role was expressed in the mission of the SEC: "to protect investors, maintain fair, orderly, and efficient markets, and facilitate capital formation". In the opinion of the author, the 2007-2009 financial crisis has demonstrated that this traditional view of the purposes of securities regulation is far too limited. Securities regulation must now be in the front line of efforts to preserve the stability of the financial system, within economies and globally. The independence of securities regulators should be preserved. In the stability area, elected legislators must set objectives and standards, while regulators should be free to apply that policy across different segments of the industry and in changing financial conditions. Legislators typically favour rules-based regulation, in order to guard against the exercise of arbitrary power by unelected regulators. It is, however, a challenge to frame a regulatory regime and policies that are flexible, capable of dynamic adjustment so as to help preserve stability, but also legitimate and consistent with statutory mandates. A regime of constrained discretion might be the best solution. The internationalization of finance represents also a challenge for securities regulation. National policy makers have to cooperate with their foreign counterparts. The author argues in favor of a combination of minimum international standards

---

[1]   Director, Research and Statistics Department, CNMV.
[2]   Counsel to the Board and Head, Economic Analysis Division, OeNB and SUERF Secretary General.
[3]   Professor Emeritus of Finance, Aarhus University.

and some form of mutual recognition. Regulators need to be open with legislators about the international component of their policy making. It falls to legislatures to oversee, with sustained interest and vigour, regulatory agencies' stewardship of the regime. All that needs to be done without undermining disclosure-enforcement, the traditional core of securities regulation, as the key to honest and fair markets.

In chapter 3, *Michael Haliassos*, Chair for Macroeconomics and Finance, Goethe University Frankfurt and Director for the Center for Financial Studies, analyses "Challenges in designing investor and borrower protection". The author mentions two possible alternatives to regulation: Financial education and financial advice. However, the impact of education on financial performance is uncertain, and financial advice may be biased because of conflicts of interest. So, after all regulation might be appropriate. Product-based regulation should concern attributes and levels of disclosure. Product complexity may interfere with the potential for disclosure. User-based regulation might be criticized as paternalistic or discriminatory. The author recommends that financial advisors should be certified for having the appropriate level of expertise to perform their role. When advisors have a dual role as sellers and providers of guidance, conflicts of interest arise. The introduction of 'fee-only' advisors in Germany in 2014 was based on the idea of separating the roles of seller and advice provider. A further idea is to require each financial product to have its own 'passport' that potential users can consult and keep as a standard reference. The optimal solution seems to be to bundle regulation together with other measures.

In chapter 4, *Theodor Kockelkoren*, Member of the Executive Board, AFM, and Chairman OECD Task Force on Financial Consumer Protection, discusses "Protecting financial consumers and retail products: a case for smart intervention and better information". The author argues that we should be humble when it comes to expecting a major impact from ever more information to financial consumers. Long prospectuses written in legalese are ordinary investors not able to understand. In the Netherlands in 2013, an inducement ban was introduced concerning incentives from product manufacturers to advisors or other distributors in order to have their products sold to customers. It has already had positive effects. The inducement ban has increased pricing differentiation. Execution only customers now pay lower fees. Customers also have access to a broader range of services. Competition between product manufacturers has increased. Distributors are now focusing more on customers' needs. Execution only and tied advice have, however, been exempted from the inducement ban in MiFID 2, and this could mean that both may gain ground at the expense of independent advice and portfolio management.

In chapter 5, *Juan Carlos Ureta*, President Renta4 and President Fundación de Estudios Financieros discusses "Beyond information: the role of banks and financial entities in educating investors". In the view of the author, complex and comprehensive information about financial products is of limited value in protection of retail investors. It is much more effective to give investors financial education. It is important to give financial products names that are not misleading. The need for financial education is particularly obvious in an environment of zero interest rates on safe assets. Investors should understand that search for yield implies acceptance of risk. It is, however, difficult to understand the risk implications of investing in complex financial products. He uses the expression that investors should know that 'Eldorado' does not exist. Integrating financial education into business models should be a priority for financial institutions and the financial industry as a whole.

In chapter 6, *José Manuel González-Páramo*, BBVA, Member of the Board of Directors, Chief Officer, Global Economics, Regulation & Public Affairs, explains "The role of banks in fostering financial inclusion". Financial literacy has been found to be very low around the world. The combination of more complex financial products and insufficient financial capability has played a role in recent financial crises. Financial service providers should contribute to promoting financial literacy. Not only individuals can benefit from improved financial literacy. Also banks and other financial institutions can benefit. Financial literacy has the potential to increase the demand for savings products. Financial literacy may also have a positive impact on customers' debt management. At the aggregate level, financial literacy may contribute to preserve the stability and soundness of the financial system as a whole. Financially literate consumers are likely to exert stronger market discipline on banks and consequently enhance the efficiency of the financial sector. All in all, banks have enormous incentives for contributing to financial education, apart from corporate social responsibility. It is not just a moral responsibility towards the societies where they operate, but also a consistent investment in their business sustainability.

In chapter 7, *Lori J. Schock*, Director, Office of Investor Education and Advocacy, US Securities and Exchange Commission (SEC) describes "The role of regulators in investor education". In the mid-1990s, SEC began to focus in earnest on investor education. The aim is to help US investors obtain the fundamental information they need to make informed investment decisions and avoid fraud. In 2009, the SEC launched Investor.gov, its first-ever website focused exclusively on investor education. Key resources from the website are also included in the Financial Literacy and Education Commission's financial education website, MyMoney.gov. SEC offers also printed publications. Another way the SEC reaches out to individual investors is through Investor Alerts and Bulletins.

Investors are warned about potentially questionable activity. SEC has formed partnerships with government agencies and private institutions in order to encourage investment literacy. In addition, SEC handles investment-related complaints and questions from the public.

In chapter 8, *Colin Mayer*, Peter Moores Professor of Management Studies, Saïd Business School, University of Oxford, writes about "The risk of risk committees". In recent years, several important financial markets have been manipulated, and regulators have failed to identify evidence of this in pricing patterns. The main regulatory response to the failures of financial institutions during the financial crisis and in the market rigging cases has been to require them to have risk committees, chief risk officers and to make the boards of banks responsible for monitoring and controlling risks. The author asks, if this is the right approach. With reference to the organization, compensation policy, ownership structure and performance of the Swedish bank Handelsbanken, the author argues that the answer is no. Conventional views about corporate governance simply do not apply in relation to either specific examples or evidence from empirical studies of large numbers of banks. It is difficult to monitor risks centrally. Too centralized risk committees discourage banks from doing what they should be doing. If risk control is regarded a primary objective and banks are penalized for taking it by being required to hold capital in proportion to their risk-weighted assets then they stop taking risks. Risk committees should be involved in the banks' strategy to avoid excessive concentrations of activity, to provide early warning of developing risk concentrations and in formulating hedging principles, but that is very different from saying that the purpose of a risk committee is to control risk. There is not a right way or a single form of corporate governance.

In chapter 9, Eddy *Wymeersch*, Professor, University of Gent discusses "Corporate governance of banks according to the CRD IV". The author gives an overview of recent EU legislation concerning corporate governance of financial institutions. After the financial crisis, governance regimes have been changed from private law into public, supervisory law. Concerns for financial risk are reflected in most of the provisions of the latest capital requirements directive. Governance is considered as a factor allowing risk to be reduced, mitigated, covered, and in general kept under control. The directive contains provisions on the structure of bank boards, board committees, internal governance, number of directorships and remuneration. The most controversial part of the directive relates to the provisions on remuneration. The objective is to break the link between remuneration and (excessive) risk taking. The author has several critical remarks on the appropriateness of the provisions.

In her opening remarks at the start of the conference, *Elvira Rodriguez*, Chairperson, CNMV told the audience that the organizers wanted to give the invited international experts the opportunity to evaluate the current state of affairs in securities markets regulation in general and in investor protection, financial literacy and education and corporate governance in particular. The chapters in the present SUERF Study cover all these topics. The editors hope that the readers will find the contributions interesting and instructive.

2. FUNDAMENTAL CHALLENGES FOR SECURITIES REGULATION: A POLITICAL ECONOMY CRISIS IN THE MAKING?

Paul Tucker[1]

The announced themes of this conference are the protection of investors and corporate governance. I fear, therefore, that my address risks breaking up the party, as I shall argue that the global economic and financial crisis has put it beyond reasonable doubt that the traditional view of the purposes of securities regulation is far too limited. Securities regulators have to be actively involved in preserving financial stability, or alternatively lose some of their autonomy. Worse, I shall argue that that entails profound questions about the constitution (or institutional design) of securities regulators, their mandate and independence; about the regulatory tools and methods on which they rely; and about their involvement in international policy making. I shall review each of those three dimensions of the problem in turn after outlining the traditional mission and *modus operandi* of securities regulators.

In doing so, I do not mean to criticize securities regulators in general or any specific agencies in particular, and throughout I shall adopt the European approach of taking 'securities regulation' to include the regulation of derivatives products and markets[2].

2.1. SECURITIES REGULATION AS TRADITIONALLY CONCEIVED AND PRACTICED, AND WHY IT IS NO LONGER ENOUGH

Once upon a time, securities regulators policed the integrity of individual transactions and offerings on public exchanges served by specialized intermediaries. The intermediaries were typically small, and the key public policy interest in them was that they be sufficiently liquid to be wound down in an orderly way if they got into difficulty. That wasn't the hardest thing in the world to deliver. More demanding was how to ensure that markets were fair, that the public wasn't ripped off or defrauded. To meet that challenge, the central tenet of the US's

---

[1]   Harvard Kennedy School and Harvard Business School.
[2]   Indeed, I remain grateful for the help of then commissioners and staff of the SEC and the CFTC when, following the 1987 stock market crash, I spent a period in Hong Kong helping to redesign its securities market infrastructure and, in particular, what became the Securities and Futures Commission. See the Report of the Hong Kong Securities Review Committee, 1988.

Securities and Exchange Commission (SEC) was disclosure-enforcement[3]. Issuers of securities were expected to disclose all information materially relevant to investors. And pre-trade and post-trade transparency was required to make secondary markets fair.

This was a world where the key lever of the securities regulator was the power to enforce the law, whether administrative injunction, administrative fine or (acting through departments of justice) via prosecution brought in the courts. The securities regulator's central task was, accordingly, the adjudication of individual cases, whether or not action proceeded to the criminal justice system.

Separately from their enforcement activities, regulators approved, overrode or substituted for the rules of securities exchanges and market bodies, essentially self-regulating trade associations. Often that role would entail balancing the varying interests of different groups of participants in the capital markets, such as corporate issuers, small intermediaries, big intermediaries, fund managers, and so on. Although not a universal truth, rarely were the issues in this second area of activity seen as being of first-order importance for the public, and even more rarely were they salient. The regulators' role in writing or approving rules was, therefore, widely seen as a technical arena in which it acted as a kind of umpire between competing interest groups.

That overall mission, and the culture it fostered, remained intact at most securities regulators even as, over the decades, their mandate was extended beyond public exchanges to over-the-counter markets, to private placements, to fund management, and to clearing and settlement systems. The watchword was disclosure, and the key instrument was enforcement. On the whole, that prioritization proved popular with legislative overseers, especially in the US, as bringing wrong-doers to book was readily understood and supported by the public. For many years that salience underpinned the public status of securities regulators. It harnessed their interest in their own reputation and standing to one particular public concern: honesty and fairness in financial services.

How the crisis changes all that

There was a wobble in this set up after the 1987 stock market crash, since that was a national and international *economic* event rather than a problem of opacity or of wickedness *per se*. But in spite of a raft of reports around the world, including most famously that of the Brady Commission in the USA, the crash did not, in the end, give rise to a fundamental rethink of the purposes and modalities of securities regulation. For example, in the US the mission of the SEC, as

---

[3]   A.M. KHADEMIAN, *The SEC and Capital Market Regulation: the Politics of Expertise*, 1992.

expressed in its annual strategy statement, has remained "to protect investors; maintain fair, orderly, and efficient markets; and facilitate capital formation"[4]. Echoes of that can be found in the statutory objectives of the UK's new Financial Conduct Authority, which are "to secure an appropriate degree of protection for consumers; to protect and enhance the integrity of the UK financial system; to promote effective competition in the interests of consumers"[5].

The latest crisis poses a much more fundamental challenge than the 1987 crash to the traditional conception of market regulation I have been describing. Indeed, it alters that picture fundamentally.

The depth and severity of the initial crisis in 2007-2009, followed by only slow and stuttering macroeconomic recovery, underline the vital social importance of stability. But that is not a remotely a project that can fall solely to macroeconomic policymakers and bank supervisors. Although banking reform has often seemed centre stage, it has by no means been the exclusive focus of attention. A few examples will illustrate this.

There's reform underway of derivatives markets, secured money markets (usually known as repo markets), securities-lending markets, securitization markets, central counterparty clearing houses, credit rating agencies[6]. These reforms are addressed to some of the economy's main capital markets: their structure and the terms under which participants meet and trade. In most countries, they fall under the jurisdiction not of central banks and bank supervisors, but of securities regulators. That's to say, the European Securities and Markets Authority for the EU as a whole; the Financial Conduct Authority in London; and the Securities and Exchange Commission and the Commodities and Futures Trading Commission in the US.

And then there's an area that blurs the boundaries of banking and markets regulation: 'shadow banking'. These are firms, funds or structures that as a matter of law are typically not caught by banking legislation and regulation, but which have the economic substance of banks in that they borrow short term to fund illiquid loans to households and businesses. As such, they are, like banks, exposed to the risk of runs, possibly forcing them into bankruptcy and bringing about a contraction in the supply of credit to the economy, hurting more or less everyone. In other words, they can cause systemic distress. In this realm too, which I should note by no means extends to the whole of market-based finance, it is often securities regulators that have jurisdiction.

---

4   SEC, *The Investor's Advocate: How the SEC Protects Investors, Maintains Market Integrity, And Facilitates Capital Formation*, 2013.
5   The old Financial Services Authority paraphrased its statutory objectives as: "Market confidence; public awareness; consumer protection; reduction of financial crime".
6   For a review of the overall reform programme, see TUCKER, *Regulatory Reform, Stability, and Central Banking*, Brookings Hutchins Center, 2014.

Summing up, whether it is as regulator of securities issuance and distribution or of the terms on which derivatives are traded or of the structure of financial markets or of clearing houses or of trade repositories or of 'shadow banks' – and I could go on – securities regulation is going to be in the front line of efforts to preserve the stability of the financial system, within economies and globally[7].

As on the banking side, the reform agenda leaves market regulators with much to do. But the implications for the banking authorities and for securities regulators are, in fact, quite different. For central banks and bank supervisors, it amounts to being forcibly taken back to their roots: preserving financial stability. While that is something of a departure from, even a shock to, the culture of central banking that flourished for a decade or so prior to the crisis, they can reach back into their deep DNA as they reconfigure themselves. But for securities regulators, what is entailed is closer to requiring a transformation of mandates, regulatory techniques and decision taking. If they are now in the business of preserving financial stability, they are going to be policy makers as well as enforcement agencies, and where policy amounts to making judgments about the public interest beyond holding the ring in an interest-group bargaining process. Further, the policies needed to preserve stability unavoidably have a big international component given that global capital markets are not respecters of national boundaries. While many securities regulators have been involved in the global reform programme, I am not convinced that the implications of these changes have been widely recognized and internalized.

Against that background, I am going to articulate three challenges. First, how to validate and frame the independence of securities regulators. Why, and to what extent, are they insulated from politics? As their mandates evolve, should they remain independent? Second, can a reliance on detailed rule books, the stock-in-trade of regulatory policy for markets, deliver what society needs to preserve financial stability? And if not, can regulatory discretion be squared with agency independence? Third, to what extent can national securities regulators, and the national legislatures that created and oversee them, make policy independently of each other? And to the extent that some policymaking is unavoidably a collective international enterprise, how can securities regulatory policy enjoy democratic legitimacy?

I believe that if these issues are not recognized and addressed, sooner or later securities regulators will find themselves torn in very different directions, creating a crisis of competence or authority, or both.

---

[7]   For my views while in office on the importance of securities regulation to stability, see TUCKER, *Building resilient financial systems: macro-prudential regimes and securities market regulation*, Bank of England, May 2011.

That is not merely the perspective of a former central banker. In a recent lecture delivered in New York SEC Commissioner Daniel Gallagher addressed similar issues from a different perspective: "...the US capital markets, the manner in which they are regulated, and the SEC itself collectively face an existential threat: the encroaching imposition of so-called prudential regulation on markets wholly unsuited to that regulatory paradigm"[8]. Dan and I agree that this is a pressing set of issues.

A few years ago, the International Organization of Securities Commissions (IOSCO), a body to which I shall return when discussing my third challenge, agreed by consensus amongst its entire global membership to amend its high-level Principles to add a new provision that securities-regulator mandates should include stability as an objective[9]. Implementation is, shall we say, patchy[10].

2.2. THE INDEPENDENCE OF SECURITIES REGULATORS: CHANGING MISSIONS WITHOUT CHANGING MANDATES

For roughly a century in the US, and for a rather shorter period in Europe, democratically elected governments have been hiving off areas of public policy and delegating them to agencies that are 'independent' in the sense of being insulated, to a greater or lesser extent, from day-to-day politics.

Apart from political expediency – such as shifting blame, or the legislature limiting the power of the executive government, or just following fashion – it is sometimes less than clear, however, why power is delegated to agencies led by unelected officials. That matters because 'independence' is not a monolith but comes in different varieties, the design of agencies reflecting how legislators choose to balance 'insulation' and 'democratic control' given the regime's original purpose and mission.

---

[8]   D.M. GALLAGHER, *The 15th Annual A A Sommer Jr. Lecture on Corporate, Securities and Financial Law*, 16 October 2014.

[9]   IOSCO Principles 6 and 7 were added in 2010. They are, respectively, "The Regulator should have or contribute to a process to monitor, mitigate and manage systemic risk, appropriate to its mandate" and "The Regulator should have or contribute to a process to review the perimeter of regulation regularly". The incorporation of "contribute to" is weak unless there exists a separate body with a well-articulated remit to preserve stability and a rounded set of powers, including in markets regulation.

[10] In the UK, the 'integrity' objective of the FCA is elaborated in the statute in a way that gives a hook for financial stability, and the Financial Policy Committee of the Bank of England can give the FCA comply-or-explain Recommendations and, in some areas, binding Directions, so long as the required action is within the market regulator's vires. In the USA, interestingly the preamble to the SEC's key governing legislation motivates the need for the agency very broadly, including the need for a more effective national banking system and Federal Reserve System, and the risk of sudden and unreasonable fluctuations in the prices of securities causing alternately unreasonable expansion and unreasonable contraction of the volume of credit supplied to the economy. That captures a good deal of modern thinking about why financial stability matters but it is not fleshed out in the body of the legislation, nor in the SEC's own mission statement.

For securities regulation *as traditionally conceived*, the normative case for independence – although rarely set out – has amounted to a variant of the case for the courts and for the central prosecuting authorities being insulated from the influence of day-to-day politics. Justice is being administered. Apparent attempts by the Nixon Administration to intervene in SEC cases in the early-1970s underlined the need for insulation from politics. In a similar vein, insulation – both from political parties *and* from industry capture – is useful if the regulator's role in rule-writing amounts to that of a neutral umpire holding the ring amongst competing sectional interests.

The case for independence in financial stability policy is, however, rather different. It is less about the adjudication of individual cases than it is about designing the rules of the game for finance as a whole. Further, precisely because the problem of financial stability is about spillovers (or negative externalities) from private sector behaviour, industry input to policy making, however diverse, is unlikely to capture the social costs of distress. And because those costs are broadly spread across society as a whole and because the issues are so technical, public input during peacetime, before it is too late, is either unlikely or relatively ill-informed or both. Indeed, in the short run the public might like a boom, with its easier credit availability for borrowers, and appreciating asset values for investors. Regulatory policy in the pursuit of stability entails making (and openly debating) judgments about the public interest and about operating a consistent policy even when faced with the short-term temptations of allowing (or even of generating) a boom. If that sounds more like the case for an independent monetary authority, we should not be surprised. Both revolve around the advantages to society of neutralizing the incentive of politicians to generate booms in order to boost their popularity before the costs become apparent.

An important question, therefore, is whether securities regulators have been designed with the *kind* of independence suited to the pursuit of a mandate to preserve systemic stability. I think not.

In common with too many other independent regulatory agencies, securities regulators often have statutory objectives that are, to put it mildly, vague. For example, the SEC is responsible, amongst other things, for "the protection of investors". But it is not clear how *much* protection the enacting legislator thought is required.

Consistent with that, Congress retained considerable residual control. The US capital markets regulators are subject to the standard budgetary process, with key Congressional committees each year determining total resources and, if they wish, prescribing or proscribing, with considerable granularity, how the budget is spent. That gives them powerful indirect, as well as direct, levers over policy. It would be surprising if regulatory agencies were not sensitive to that.

Nor is the President bereft of leverage. There is a convention – not sufficiently remarked upon – that upon a change of Administration, the chair of a regulatory body offers her or his resignation to the incoming President. Although commissioners cannot be fired without cause and so *do* each enjoy some independence, this convention effectively means that the President can ensure that the overall direction of the agency is in sympathetic hands given that the chair leads the staff and establishes the agenda[11]. In other words, in marked contrast to monetary policy, securities regulatory policy can shift with a change in the party holding the executive branch[12].

In the US, the year-to year approach to market regulation can, therefore, be partly something of a tug of war between the executive and legislative branches. Although the modalities differ, things aren't so very different in the EU. The rules and regulations of the Securities and Markets Authority are subject to veto by the Council of Ministers and the European Parliament, and its budget is determined via a political process.

My point is not that this is bad, but that the independence of capital-markets regulators – their insulation from politics – is somewhat partial and fragile outside of their adjudicatory and enforcement roles. While that might make sense where rule-writing amounts largely to striking bargains balancing the interests of competing private sector groups, it is less suitable when the policy purpose is stability.

In summary, legislators have the wrong *kind* of political control if securities regulators are to play their part in preserving stability: closer to tactical than to strategic control. What is needed in the stability area is a standard set by elected legislators (after due public debate), with regulators free to apply that policy across different segments of the industry and in changing financial conditions. That way, two goals can be achieved. Politicians do what only they can legitimately do in a democratic society, namely reflect and forge public preferences and objectives; and by delegating the implementation of the regime to an independent agency, the public can be insulated from the short-term incentives of elected politicians to depart from those agreed objectives in order to get re-elected by permitting exuberance liable to burst and reap havoc only at a later, uncertain date.

By bringing the regulation and supervision of capital markets fair and square within the financial stability field, the crisis challenges the political economy of the current dispensation for securities regulation, which incorporates a balance of

---

[11] As a matter of the statutory text, SEC commissioners do not enjoy explicit protection from the President firing them on a whim, but the Supreme Court has made clear that it treats them as having 'for cause' protection.

[12] That is not to say that it always does so. Both the current and previous SEC Chairs are, I believe, independents in US parlance, i.e. not affiliated to one of the two main political parties.

political and technical forces suitable for a regime established when society's goals could largely be met by a doctrine of disclosure-enforcement. Today's world is more complicated, and a richer regime is now needed for markets regulation. There has been a shift in mission without, in many jurisdictions, a legislative reform of mandates, objectives and agency design.

2.3.   STATIC RULES VERSUS *CONSTRAINED DISCRETION*: THE PROBLEMS OF A SHAPE-SHIFTING INDUSTRY AND OF EXUBERANCE

If that were not enough, there is even a question mark over whether the stock instrument for markets regulation – a *static* rule book – is suited to preserving stability. That is the second of my challenges.

Legislators typically favour rules-based regulation, in order to guard against the exercise of arbitrary power by unelected regulators. This approach is well-suited to regulation directed at market abuse. As in other areas of the law, market participants – users and intermediaries – are entitled to know where the boundaries of permissible behaviour lie.

But it is not well suited to preserving the stability of the system. A static rulebook is the meat and drink of regulatory arbitrage. The more detailed the rules and the more thoroughly the public and the industry have been consulted on drafts, the more it seems that rules-arbitrage is implicitly legitimized, because the rule-makers must have said precisely what they meant and no more.

This problem is endemic because finance is a 'shape-shifter'. The essentials of a banking business can be constructed in a non-bank; a derivatives business could be written as a portfolio of insurance policies; and so on.

That makes it hard to frame a regime that keeps risk-taking in the system as a whole within tolerable bounds. Excessive risk taking is likely to migrate to less regulated or unregulated parts of the system. Thus, with the re-regulation of *de jure* banks currently underway, some of the economic substance of banking will, again, inevitably re-emerge elsewhere, in what is known as shadow banking.

Of course, this is not a new problem. The role of structured investment vehicles, asset-backed securitizations, commercial paper conduits and money market funds, each of them regulated to some extent, in cracking the financial ceiling in 2007 is well documented. That many of the most excessive structures have since been in retreat doesn't mean the general phenomenon has gone away. Anybody holding low-risk securities can, in principle, build themselves a shadow bank by lending-out ('repo-ing') their securities for cash and investing the proceeds in a riskier credit portfolio. And they can do so very quickly. Sometimes, their liquidity fragility and the systemic significance of their collapse will be identified only *ex post*.

Up to a point, this can be addressed through the regulation of institutions. If, say, an insurance company reinvents itself as a *de facto* banking and derivatives business, it could in principle be subjected to banking-like regulation of liquidity and leverage risk[13]. But banking-like fragility can also be generated through Russian doll-like chains of transactions or structures, via which *aggregate* leverage and/or liquidity mismatches *gradually* accumulate, without involving individual financial firms that could be re-labelled and regulated as banks.

This shape-shifting dynamic can leave policymakers in a game of catch-up, responding only as each incarnation becomes systemically significant – next year, or perhaps even right now, who knows what: real-estate investment trusts, credit funds, leveraged exchange-traded funds? That is a game that sooner or later the authorities are doomed to lose, with potentially cataclysmic consequences. By the time the products of regulatory arbitrage are evidently systemically significant, those in the driving street will likely have the lobbying power to delay reform. The debates around the reform of the US money market fund industry illustrate that in capital letters.

Nor is it only a problem of regulatory arbitrage. It is also hard to frame a regime that can cater for the tendency of financial markets to pass from a normal pattern of risk-taking to exuberance and then, after the euphoria blows itself out, to depressed risk-taking. As we have seen, those violent swings are not conducive to effective capital formation across the credit and business cycle. Static minimum regulatory requirements – e.g. for counterparty credit risk – could in theory be calibrated for the most exuberant risk environment, but that could adversely affect credit supply in normal conditions. This being so, static requirements calibrated to 'normal' are not going to prove enough if and when the system moves to 'exuberant'. In other words, a capacity for *dynamic* adjustment of regulatory requirements has to be introduced into such regimes, in order to *maintain* the desired degree of systemic resilience across different risk environments.

The challenge, therefore, and it is a serious one, is to frame a regulatory regime and policies that are flexible, capable of dynamic adjustment so as to help preserve stability, but also legitimate and consistent with statutory mandates.

This almost certainly entails granting greater discretion to regulatory agencies charged with preserving stability, which I have argued must include regulation of

---

[13] Subsidiaries of AIG are reported to have done just that in the run up to the 2007-08 part of the crisis, but without banking-type or stability-oriented supervision and regulation.

capital markets as well as of banks. For example, regulators need to be able to vary minimum collateral (margin, haircut) requirements in derivatives and money markets when a cyclical upswing is morphing into exuberance; they need to be able to tighten the regime applying to a corner of finance that is shifting from systemic irrelevance to a systemic threat; they need to be able to tighten the substantive standards, not only the disclosure standards, applying to the issuance of securities when the pattern of *aggregate* issuance is driving or facilitating excessive borrowing by firms or households. They need, moreover, to be able to take each of those measures promptly, before it is too late. And so they need the information to make, explain and defend those judgments in public. Given the scope of their jurisdiction over capital markets, securities regulators will be in the middle of all that.

But the keys of the kingdom cannot be handed over to unelected bureaucrats! This points to a regime of *constrained discretion*. The objective should be clear; the instruments should be clear; there should be provision for dynamic adjustment where warranted to meet the objective. That, of course, sounds rather more like the monetary policy regimes developed over the past quarter century than traditional securities regulation (or indeed prudential supervision). Those degrees of constrained discretion are alien to securities regulation as it has evolved over nearly a century. The choices, crudely, are twofold.

One option would be that some other body be granted the power to override and set capital markets policy where that was demonstrably warranted in the interests of stability. In the UK, the Bank of England Financial Policy Committee, on which the chief executive of the securities regulator (FCA) has a vote, has something approximating that role: reflecting the express intent of Parliament, the UK's new statutory regime is explicitly macro-prudential. The FPC's nearest analogue in the US is the Financial Services Oversight Council, established by the Dodd Frank Act but which, to date, has not been hugely popular with all SEC and CFTC commissioners. The second option, therefore, is to introduce more degrees of freedom for securities regulators, under a new statutory objective of preserving stability and active Congressional oversight of that function. As I have argued already, that too would entail a substantial change in remit, mindset, agency design and accountability.

2.4.   NATIONAL VERSUS INTERNATIONAL POLICY-MAKING: ARE THERE STILL *NATIONAL* CAPITAL MARKETS?

My third challenge for the political economy of securities regulation stems from the internationalization of finance.

Just as once upon a time securities regulation was entirely separate from banking supervision and financial stability, so once upon a time 'national' capital markets were neatly segmented. That world lies in the distant past. After all, London's multi-currency Euromarkets got going again nearly half a century ago, as developed economies progressively relaxed controls on capital flows. But the full implications of global capital markets for policy making (and for enforcement) have been obscured for a long time.

A decade ago, international-relations theorists argued that economic policy making was increasingly centred on international organisations of various kinds, such as IOSCO which I have mentioned already, the Basel process, the IMF, the WTO[14]. But things aren't always what they seem. Until recently at least, Basel and IOSCO have differed materially in how much they affect their member institutions and countries.

It is a true bill that significant policy initiatives have for decades been taken by central bankers and bank supervisors in Basel. With an internationalist outlook that arguably has its roots in the 19th century gold standard and the mid-20th century Bretton Woods monetary regime, central bankers have long recognized that the costs of bank failures in one country can all too easily spill over into other countries. That much had been clear in the 1930s when Creditanstalt failed in Vienna, but the Governors were given a painful reminder when Bankhaus Herstatt failed in 1974 with outstanding foreign-exchange transactions that were only half-settled when the music stopped. As barriers to international banking were dismantled in the 1970s and '80s, the Governors found it natural to try to agree common minimum standards to solve the collective action problems they faced, reaching decisions by consensus and with a reasonably strong cultural barrier to individual supervisors holding out unreasonably. This was and is a world where even the most powerful countries can find it in their interests – in the interests of their citizens – to compromise in order to achieve a stronger common international standard for all than some would adopt on their own[15].

Although it shares with the Basel Supervisors Committee the form of a 'transnational regulatory organisation'[16], for much of its life IOSCO did not in fact operate in the same way. In the world of securities regulation, IOSCO was for many years really a forum for exchanging views rather than for agreeing common minimum standards. Thus, the scene was set for the SEC to find it

---

[14]   Notably, A.-M. SLAUGHTER, *A New World Order*, 2004.
[15]   To be clear, the failure of the Basel Supervisors Committee prior to the latest crisis was that its capital standard was substantively flawed.
[16]   A concept coined by R.O. KEOHANE and J.S. NYE Jr, *Transgovernmental Relations and International Organizations*, 1974, which as it happens was the year the decision to create the Basel Supervisors Committee was taken.

difficult when IOSCO, supported by the G20 Financial Stability Board, agreed a policy on the regulation of money market funds that some US commissioners opposed. In the wake of the crisis, IOSCO's role and purpose in international economic life was changing, and that came as a bit of a shock. Suddenly, its endeavours – its work programme and outputs – were being scrutinized by G20 finance ministers and Leaders, with the FSB an intermediary between the politicians and the technical specialists. It is not surprising that some of the IOSCO membership blinked as global securities regulators emerged into the sunlight. After all, IOSCO policy had in practice been dominated by the longest established and most seasoned agencies. As the issues they are responsible for gained public salience around the world and as emerging-market economies became more important in the global economy and balance of power, the *modus operandi* of IOSCO policy-making seemed to be changing, confronting national regulators with challenges on how to determine the lines they should take at international fora, and what to do if they could not get everything they wanted.

To a greater or lesser extent, national securities regulators tend to hold onto two propositions. The first is that markets are still essentially national. That is largely untrue. The second is that they are empowered by and are accountable to their national legislatures, which expect them to protect their national citizenry. That, of course, is not only accurate, it is vitally important for generating and sustaining democratic legitimacy. But what national policy makers cannot maintain is that they are able to deliver on their national mandates without cooperating actively with their foreign counterparts. Without imposing capital controls, even the largest economies in the world cannot insulate themselves from problems in poorly regulated foreign financial systems.

This has given rise to an environment where some national regimes and regulators seek extraterritorial effect for their rules. For example, in the US the Dodd Frank Act laid down that CFTC regulations on derivatives should apply abroad when cross-border activities have a "direct and significant connection with activities in, or effect on, commerce in the United States". The CFTC has since published hundreds of pages of interpretation, and has been locked in negotiations with its counterparts. I find it hard to see this as a sustainable equilibrium if anything like the current global order is to be sustained. Oversimplifying, the reaction to the CFTC trying to apply some of their derivatives policy beyond the borders of the US has been for the EU to turn the tables on the US in a related sphere where the US regime was weaker. Asia watches and waits.

The issues run deep. Hypothetically, should the US, the issuer of the world's main reserve currency, seek jurisdiction over a dollar-denominated transaction outside the US between two non-US domiciled entities, on the grounds that the transfer of dollars must ultimately be effected within the United States? For those inclined to answer 'yes', can I suggest that we also need to answer the reciprocal question of whether the sovereign issuer of some new reserve currency should have jurisdiction over trades in that currency transacted between entities in, say, California and Massachusetts. And what would the network of extraterritorial jurisdictional claims look like if and when, as in the latter part of the 19th century, we gradually move into a world monetary system with plural reserve currencies?

That, I would suggest, is a world where a combination of minimum international standards and some form of mutual recognition has attractions for all states. That is what the key US and European regulators have been attempting, but it was striking that CFTC, SEC and the EU initially set out with quite different conceptions of what mutual recognition or 'substituted compliance' should comprise. Line-by-line equivalence, output equivalence, or what[17]?

This is also a world where international standard-setters need the wherewithal to check national delivery of (compliance with) those standards, as Basel is now pursuing on its bank-capital regimes.

Further, it is a world where regulators, and indeed the executive branch of government, need to be open with legislators about the international component of their policy making. And it is a world where those legislators need to be open with the citizens they represent about how they factor international spillovers and policy making into their casting and oversight of domestic regimes[18].

None of that will be easy, and in some respects it is, again, alien to securities regulators and also to their overseers in national legislatures. But what is not remotely alien to them is protecting investors, and that is increasingly a shared, cross-border effort as, taken as a whole, investors hardly gain from systemic crises.

2.5.   CONCLUSION

The public, and businesses, desperately need to be confident that financial stability can be restored and preserved. Given open capital markets and endemic regulatory arbitrage, that is unavoidably a shared and interdependent venture between, amongst others, central bankers and securities regulators. My purpose

---

[17]   In July 2013, IOSCO announced that it was establishing a Task Force on Cross-Border Regulation, chaired by Ashley Adler of the Hong Kong Securities and Futures Commission. This picks up and broadens issues identified within the SEC a few years earlier: E. TAFARA and R.J. PETERSON, "A Blueprint for Cross-Border Access to US Investors: A New International Framework", *Harvard International Law Journal*, Winter 2007.

[18]   For a more extended treatment of whether it is possible to square international standard setting by groups of independent agencies with democratic legitimacy, see TUCKER, *Reforming the International Monetary and Financial System: What Role For National Democracies?*, Peterson Institute of International Economics, Washington DC, 12 December 2014.

here has not at all been to imply that central banks and banking supervisors can escape their share of responsibility. Of course they cannot. But this is *not* a competition between regulatory communities with different traditions and mindsets: either for turf or for self-mortification.

As I have attempted to explain, I doubt whether the current configuration of securities regulators' mandates and powers is fully adequate to preserving stability. There are challenges from the way objectives are framed, from the prospect that static rule-books are doomed to fail, and from cross-border spillovers making essential not only co-operation but also a degree of shared policy-making.

Securities regulators are signaling that they are grappling with some of these issues. Steven Maijoor, the chair of ESMA, has spoken publicly on stability quite frequently. Recently, Mary Jo White, chair of the SEC, did so too in a wide-ranging discussion of the regulation of the asset management industry[19].

I think a robust solution would be regime of 'constrained discretion'. That would entail material changes in legislative regimes and agency design, with more carefully articulated statutory objectives and greater transparency in decision-taking substituting, in some jurisdictions, for more hands-on forms of democratic control.

That would need to be delivered in ways that preserve to elected politicians the essential democratic role of setting objectives and the standard of resilience society demands. If they don't set the standard for the system's desired resilience, then independent regulators are by default making high policy. That doesn't seem right. By involving finance ministries and reporting to G20 Leaders, the Financial Stability Board helps to address this crucial issue.

With standards of resilience set in this way, it then falls to legislatures to oversee, with sustained interest and vigour, regulatory agencies' stewardship of the regime. That must mean regular oversight, not just politicians responding to 'fire alarms' set off by constituents or interest groups with a grievance. Fire alarms can be horribly late when it comes to the public's need for financial stability.

All that needs to be done without undermining disclosure-enforcement, the traditional core of securities regulation, as the key to honest and fair markets.

That is quite an agenda, but it is unavoidable.

---

[19]   M.J. WHITE, Chair of the US Securities and Exchange Commission, *Enhancing Risk Monitoring and Regulatory Safeguards for the Asset Management Industry*, 11 December 2014. This was delivered after my talk at the SUERF/CNMV conference in November but before the published version of my remarks was finalized.

3. CHALLENGES IN DESIGNING INVESTOR AND BORROWER PROTECTION

Michael Haliassos[1]

> *"The basic mission of finance is to set up arrangements whereby people may pursue risky opportunities without themselves being destroyed by this risk, and arrangements that incentivize people to behave in a socially constructive manner."*
>
> Robert Shiller (2012)

3.1. THE NEED FOR REGULATION

In today's world, with social security systems unable to provide adequate pension benefits, financial innovation bombarding households with new and advanced products, and a serious need for households to build (or knit!) elaborate asset/debt portfolios, it is fair to ask if regulation is needed, in order to protect the interests of investors and borrowers. Regulation presupposes a potential for abuse of power by suppliers and/or misuse of products by households. However, it also limits free will, makes at least some people worse off than they would otherwise be, and requires expertise for proper guidance.

There is no shortage of proposed alternatives to regulation. Why not educate households, so that they can make their own informed choices? Why not rely on their access to financial advice and willingness to use it? Why not simply provide information, through massive campaigns such as that of Margaret Thatcher in the 1980s, which led to a dramatic increase in stock market participation and lived up to the conservative politician's dream of turning workers into capitalists?

All these sound plausible ideas, but the jury is still out on whether they work effectively. For example, we know that the less financially literate also tend to be less likely to be prepared for retirement and to participate in the stock market. But which way does it go? Could it be that people first decide to prepare for retirement, for whatever reason, and then read up to familiarize themselves with interest compounding and real versus nominal interest rates; or that they do both for other reasons that we don't observe or control? In either of these cases, there is no guarantee that exogenously providing additional financial education would improve retirement planning. Moreover, establishing causality is only one step in

---

[1]   Goethe University Frankfurt, CFS and SAFE, CEPR, NETSPAR.

the meandering road to informed outcomes through an optimally designed education program.

Conflicts of interest in financial advice are yet another example of factors potentially calling for some intervention and control. Indeed, in a 2012 paper with Hackethal and Jappelli, we found that, if one controls for investor characteristics, advised accounts exhibit worse risk-return tradeoffs (lower Sharpe ratios) than unadvised accounts, both in a brokerage setting with independent financial advisors and in a bank setting with bank employees providing advice.

Financial products share many features with drugs. A particular asset or debt product is not necessarily suitable for all, it may harm in inappropriate doses, it may not be known to those for whom it is suitable, and it may not be even available in places familiar to potential investors and borrowers. Yet, financial products are even more likely to be misused than drugs. It is hard to print the right 'dosage' on the box, or to convince people to pay the same attention as they do with drugs. Investors and borrowers fear for their lives more than they fear financial disasters, and they take doctors much more seriously than financial advisors. James Tobin used to say that economists are very unfortunate people. If they say something with which others agree, others think it is trivial. If they say something with which others disagree, the others simply think that economists are wrong.

So, maybe we need to consider regulation because other approaches do not work, at least fully. However, this is not enough: we cannot award the prize to the second piano player simply after hearing the first! We need to check instead that the second competitor, in our case regulation, performs the task well. In other words, we need to figure out on what basis we could regulate and how far each alternative would take us.

I can think of four main aspects on which to base regulation aimed at investor/borrower protection: the financial product itself, the relevant characteristics of the user, the background and compensation scheme of financial advisors, and the information provided by producers of the financial product. Listing the factors is much easier than implementing them.

3.2.   PRODUCT-BASED REGULATION

Bob Shiller rightly insists that financial theory can and should be used as a basis for designing financial products. However, the theoretically optimal or expected use of a product may have little to do with how it is actually used. Moreover, like nitrogen and glycerin, individually innocuous products can become lethal when used in combination. Bob Merton often makes the point that lowering of interest rates, improving the potential to refinance mortgages, and introducing home equity loans (to allow homeowners to liquidate some of their real estate wealth without selling their homes) were all great developments individually. Yet, they provided in combination an important building block of the US subprime crisis.

Past use of an instrument, whether in the same or in a different type of account, should also not be assumed for future use; and even if it could be assumed, cumulation of adverse financial consequences cannot be ruled out. There is no reason to suppose that households trading (or possibly overtrading) stocks individually or through mutual funds will follow the same strategy when they put those stocks in retirement accounts serving a different objective. In fact, in a 2010 paper with Bilias and Georgarakos, we showed that, although US households with brokerage accounts traded stocks intensively, trading stocks in other types of accounts paled in comparison; and that even brokerage customers typically put less than 10% of their financial assets in such accounts.

There is a legal perspective to implementation of product-based regulation: products could be restricted if their attributes interfere with the legally required minimum levels of disclosure. Complex structured products come to mind as a possible example of a characteristic (complexity) that interferes with the potential for disclosure. Indeed, Belgium recently banned sales of complex structured products to consumers. The example becomes even more compelling if we recognize that complexity can often be an avoidable feature of a financial product but a deliberate choice by producers, as it tends to be associated with larger hidden markups (see Celerier and Vallee, 2014, for evidence in this regard).

3.3.   USER-BASED REGULATION

Let us turn to user-based regulation. The basic premise here is that households with certain characteristics or revealed behavior would over-expose themselves to specific financial products if allowed to do so, and therefore we need regulation in order to constrain them. It is not hard to criticize this view, at best as paternalistic and at worst as discriminatory. The latter perception can be strengthened by the realization that previous experience with using a product is likely to require personal use of that product; and that access may not be equal regardless of user characteristics even in the absence of user-based regulation.

Yet, there are two further reasons to be skeptical. The first arises from the finding of Campbell, Calvet, and Sodini (2007) that greater financial sophistication is not always associated with smaller losses relative to an appropriate benchmark. The key here is that greater sophistication tends to encourage people to undertake greater risk exposure. In other words, although the more sophisticated face more favorable risk-return tradeoffs, they tend to take greater risks and thus experience a greater shortfall from the maximum return open to optimally behaving investors at this level of risk. By contrast, less sophisticated people tend to take less risk and to experience a smaller shortfall relative to what people of similar sophistication could optimally achieve.

The second arises from a recent finding of Fuchs-Schuendeln and Haliassos (2015). Comparing the participation behavior of East and West Germans following the event of German reunification, we found that both were equally likely to participate in 'capitalist' securities (stocks and bonds), controlling for their observable characteristics, even immediately after the opening up of the borders; and not to have any differential likelihood of exit. On the face of it, this is very surprising, because the East Germans were (exogenously) much less (if at all) familiar with these products than their West German counterparts. Yet the reason may in the end lie in the presence of a (West German) financial sector that was well familiar with those products and had healthy incentives to build a long-lasting reputation with its new clients originating from the East. If this interpretation is correct, then it suggests that lack of familiarity per se is not the criterion that regulation should exclusively focus on.

A much more relevant consideration for regulators may be whether the knowledge and structure of the supply side can make up for the lack of familiarity on the part of some users. A straightforward but rather narrow way to operationalize this may be to impose product-focused information requirements, either tailor-made for each potential investor/borrower or standardized to the requirements of the least familiar ones. Attention should also be placed, however, on whether the information provided is actually put to good use by the investor or borrower. Going from informational requirements to ensuring suitable behavior is not trivial and requires further research and design.

3.4.   REGULATION OF FINANCIAL ADVISORS

Finally, we turn to the two types of practitioners to be regulated: financial advisors and producers of financial products. As all practitioners whose advice can harm people, financial advisors need to be certified for having the appropriate level of expertise to perform their role. One could imagine a multi-level licensing approach, across products and experience. By analogy to a driver's license issued only for certain classes of vehicles, a financial advisor license could specify the classes of financial products on which they are qualified to give advice. Appropriate training and experience could be required to attain more demanding classes, in the same way that pilots are required to train on different models of aircraft, newer or bigger than the ones they have been flying, and to spend a number of hours on a flight simulator. Given the rather disappointing empirical evidence, reported in many academic studies, on advisor and analyst knowledge, ever since the first such studies were conducted in the early 1930s, such an approach to licensing could prove beneficial for all parties involved: advisors, customers, and producers.

Although driver and pilot licenses may be appealing examples, we should not forget that medical doctors and pharmacists also have to spend many long years in training, justified by the complexity of the subject and the grave potential consequences of mistakes. Interestingly, for medical practitioners we have two important enforcement mechanisms that are absent in the case of financial advisors. The first is the Hippocratic oath, and the second is an elaborate set of malpractice procedures. It is admittedly hard to imagine what could be developed in the financial sphere to mimic the Hippocratic oath. On the other hand, a framework of investor and borrower protection seems quite analogous in intent to the legal framework governing medical malpractice.

Knowledge of financial advisors is an important factor, but the structure of incentives advisors face cannot be ignored. It has long been recognized that conflicts of interest arise in the context of providing financial advice, not only between customer and advisor but also between advisor and producer of the financial product (see Inderst and Ottaviani, 2009). The former arises from the dual role of advisors as sellers and providers of guidance. The latter arises from any existing legal provisions that allow dissatisfied customers who bought financial products unsuitable for them to demand compensation by the financial advisor. It was in response to these considerations that the German government introduced the title of 'fee-only' advisors on August 1, 2014. The idea is to encourage a separation of the roles of seller and advice provider, and to allow advisors to signal such separation to customers in a credible way.

3.5. REGULATION OF PRODUCERS

Last but not least, I turn to regulation of producers. An important aspect of such regulation is a requirement of transparency, with regard to product features and risks, compensation incentives, and product suitability. For disclosure, legal provisions and procedures are well developed. A possible natural extension is to require producers to include 'nudges' in their sales documents, marketing brochures or product account statements, of the type 'consult your financial advisor'. After all, this has now become standard in medical advertising, where patients are encouraged to consult their doctor before buying even open-shelf medicines.

A further idea is to require each financial product to have its own 'passport' that potential users can consult and keep as a standard reference. There is already some evidence of ongoing research on what such a passport should include. Information on suitability for particular classes of customers and on range of possible outcomes would seem two obvious directions in which to go. Indeed, in our internet era, one could imagine this passport not as a printed booklet but as a smartphone app, which updates its contents over time and with respect to some vital characteristics of the user; or even in response to outcomes of the user with the specific product.

3.6. CONCLUSION

My overall conclusion from the discussion in this paper is that regulation is needed, but it involves a number of important challenges that cannot be ignored. Existing regulatory measures, such as disclosure and transparency requirements and introduction of fee-only financial advisors, are useful components of an appropriate regulatory framework. However, the analysis above has hopefully made clear that more thinking and a broader regulatory apparatus should be considered. For example, product access bans based on a single criterion (previous familiarity with the product) can prove counterproductive and even discriminatory in certain cases, as access is often itself a prerequisite to developing familiarity with a product. Making participation of the unfamiliar conditional on good advice or guidance by unbiased financial advisors could be considered as an alternative. Or as another example, absence of evidence of inappropriate use in the past does not guarantee good use in the future, nor does it even preclude the emergence of a crisis involving the particular product previously regarded as harmless. This should make regulators more alert and vigilant in monitoring use, but it should also not stifle innovation. This will be a difficult balance to attain.

Full development of a legal framework for investor and borrower protection is crucial, as the experience with the framework for malpractice lawsuits that supports regulation of behavior of medical practitioners illustrates. Resolving who can initiate legal action, how judgments will be passed and what are the penalties for each offense can of course be important components of such a framework, but they do not exhaust the list of design challenges. What or who exactly is to be regulated and how to verify that regulation has been effective in ensuring the protection of investor and borrower rights seem to me to be far more open-ended questions. Yet, the ultimate question is how regulation can be optimally bundled together with other measures, such as early financial education, awareness campaigns, default (i.e. automatic) options, and targeted financial advice, to improve financial behavior. We have quite a way to go before tackling this important set of issues.

References

BILIAS, Y., GEORGARAKOS, D. and HALIASSOS, M., 2010, "Portfolio Inertia and Stock Market Fluctuations", *Journal of Money, Credit and Banking* 42(4): 715-742.

CALVET, L., CAMPBELL, J.Y. and SODINI, P., 2007, "Down or Out: Assessing the Welfare Costs of Household Investment Mistakes" *Journal of Political Economy*, 115: 707-747.

CELERIER, C. and VALLEE, B., 2014, "What Drives Financial Complexity? A Look into the Retail Market for Structured Products", mimeo.

FUCHS-SCHUENDELN, N. and HALIASSOS, M., 2015, "Should Product Familiarity Be Required for Participation?", mimeo.

HACKETHAL, A., HALIASSOS, M. and JAPPELLI, T., 2012, "Financial Advisors: A Case of Babysitters?" *Journal of Banking and Finance*, 36(2): 509-524.

INDERST, R. and OTTAVIANI, M., 2009, "Misselling Through Agents" *American Economic Review*.

SHILLER, R., 2012, "Inventors in Finance: An Impressionistic History of the People Who Have Made Risk Management Work" in M. HALIASSOS (ed.), *Financial Innovation: Too Much or Too Little?*, Cambridge, MA: MIT Press.

4. PROTECTING FINANCIAL CONSUMERS AND RETAIL PRODUCTS: A CASE FOR SMART INTERVENTION AND BETTER INFORMATION

Theodor Kockelkoren[1]

4.1. INFORMATION, INTERVENTION AND INCENTIVES

Dear Ladies and Gentlemen,

Let me thank my dear hosts, the CNMV and SUERF, for inviting me to this happy occasion: 25 years of regulation and supervision by the CNMV. Feliz cumpleaños!

Perhaps your appetite has been whetted with the ambitious title *"Protecting financial consumers and retail products: a case for smart intervention and information"*. Within the short amount of time we have, I cannot do justice to the complete title, except then to present one case of a hopefully smart intervention to protect financial consumers. Before I present the case, however, we need to discuss the context of our subject.

The title of this first session today suggests that we may all feel trapped to always provide more information, in one form or another, in order to protect financial consumers. Both scientific research as practical experience teaches us that we should be humble when it comes to expecting major impact from ever more information. Naturally, we should become more clever in using our insights in how consumers behave to shape effective information requirements. Obviously, we should feel skeptical about the usefulness of 120 page prospectuses written in legalese, which – just to be utterly clear – no ordinary investor is able to understand. And appropriately, regulators using insights in behavioral science, are aiming to develop Key Information Documents that hit their target better. Still, we can only expect so much from these endeavors and that is why we – *in addition*, I should rush to underline – ought to think about other smart intervention approaches.

We can directly intervene with the products to ensure that products are in the interest of the customer group they have been designed for. For example, teaser rates in mortgage products can be restricted, difficult to understand coverage limitations in insurance can be forbidden or products that are fundamentally

---

[1] Member of the Executive Board, AfM and Chairman of the OECD Task Force on Financial Consumer Protection.

different to understand for retail customers could be banned (certain structured products fall in this category).

We can also intervene with the sales and advice practices, something which is already done in many countries. The case I wish to present to you today, in the short amount of time we have together, is about intervening to eliminate or at least significantly reduce adverse incentive structures within the financial industry. These incentive structures have been seen in the Netherlands to hold back the industry to develop products and services in the interest of its customers. Indeed, the case zooms in on banning inducements handed out by product manufacturers to advisors or other distributors in order to have their products sold to customers. The aim of the ban in the Netherlands is to enable the industry to provide their customers with high quality financial products and good quality support in their decision making.

The ban has been introduced in 2013 in the Netherlands and I have set out to present you some early experience about the impact of the ban. I will present facts as well as our impressions, using a consumer lens, first looking at services and then products. I will conclude with a brief assessment of the risks of unintended consequences.

4.2.   SERVICES

Looking at services, a striking feature of the inducement ban is the increased pricing differentiation. Previously, execution only customers in the Netherlands would pay easily 75 bp for a very narrow service, actually as much as customers that receive a fully-fledged advice in return. Since the ban, execution only customers pay no more than 25 bp. With 70% of all customers being execution only customers in the Netherlands, who collectively own 40% of the invested assets, this differentiation represents a saving of 150 million euro a year.

Another feature of the inducement ban is the increasing differentiation between service concepts. Whereas in previous times customers had two main choices: doing everything oneself (execution only) and complete bespoke advice; now, customers have more choice. Increasingly, service concepts are introduced that offer significant additional value compared to execution only, yet are not as comprehensive as bespoke advice. For example, self-directed advice tools are introduced or automated advice is experimented with. Our impression is that the ban on inducements is allowing the rapid technology developments to have their impact on financial services.

4.3.   PRODUCTS

Another impression is that with the introduction of the inducement ban, competition between product manufacturers has increased. This can be seen in the fact that some manufacturers have started to reduce prices, especially in the passive product segment. A number of manufacturers have reduced their prices by roughly 50%. This is probably in part the result of the fact that passive funds have become more popular with retail customers. In the Netherlands the share of retail invested assets allocated to passive funds roughly doubled between 2011 and 2014 – from 8% to 16%.

The increased competition between product manufacturers is probably also due to an increased sensitivity of distributors to product quality. Previously, they were keen to negotiate the most favorable distribution inducement, or retrocession. Indeed, the biggest distributors typically could extract higher inducements from asset managers than their smaller competitors. Since the inducement ban, necessarily distributors are trying to optimize their revenues in other ways. They are now focusing more on their customers, experimenting to find that mix of service concepts that best serves their customers' needs. Part and parcel of this new strategy are efficient as well as high quality investment funds. As we hear from the industry, this has fundamentally changed the discussions between asset managers and distributors.

4.4.   RISKS

Debating the merits of the inducement ban, the risk of a flight to execution only away from advice and portfolio management was discussed extensively. Two years into the ban, we can see a slight increase in the execution only customers (from 70% to 75%). At the same time, we can also see an increase in portfolio management customers (up from 6% to 11%). These increases are indeed at the expense of advice.

To be honest, these developments could be seen also well before the introduction of the ban. This is understandable, since the advice concept is ill conceived, especially in the mass market. Customers are free to deviate from the advice and, at the same time, the advisors have no way of effectively tracking these deviations. As a result, effective advice is not really possible. Also, no clear responsibility between customer and advisor is agreed on. As a result, when portfolios tank, relationships sour very quickly. It is no coincidence that the move away from advice started after the crisis hit in 2008.

To put insult to injury, the way advice typically is executed in the mass market does oftentime not pass the required quality mark. The investment objective is too often identified in very general terms. The financial position is most often only identified within the scope of the relationship with financial institution providing the advice: deposits or investments elsewhere are not taken into consideration. The identification of the ability and appetite of the client to take on risk is typically a half-baked cake: only appetite is identified – sometimes in ill-conceived ways. We made this assessment in the Dutch market by looking in detail at well over a hundred customer files. And yes, we enforce improper behavior on the level of the firm and in some cases also on individual level.

Having heard this, should we shed tears over the demise of advice? Perhaps not. However, clearly, many customers would benefit from receiving good quality support for their investment decisions. We believe, in the mass market, technology is set to play a critical role. It can realize good quality advice or support concepts at a price that suits the size of the smaller portfolios.

When it comes to tears, however, we should be forgiven if we shed a tear over the MiFID II political compromise regarding inducements. In MiFID II a ban has been introduced for independent advice as well as portfolio management. At the same time, execution only and tied advice can still receive inducements. This is not entirely different from the inducement ban in the UK, where execution only has been exempted from the ban. As a result, sales through the execution only has grown very strongly since RDR was implemented (55% in the first year and 45% in the second).

I think this should not come as a surprise, given that customers being only charged directly in the case of independent advice and portfolio management, feel that execution only is for free. Thus, we should feel worried, now that execution only and tied advice have been exempted from the inducement ban in MiFID II, both may gain ground at the expense of independent advice and portfolio management. This is quite ironical, since during the debates so much was made of the risk that customers would flee to execution only. Now, as a result of the compromise, precisely this risk may be realized.

4.5.   USE OF ADVICE

This brings me to the end of this case. If anything, I think the case makes clear that designing smart interventions is by no means easy. It requires good thinking and at the same time experimentation. In this case, the inducement in the Netherlands is perhaps an interesting experiment within the European area. It will take another two years, however, before we can seriously take stock.

5. BEYOND INFORMATION: THE ROLE OF FINANCIAL ENTITIES IN EDUCATING INVESTORS

Juan Carlos Ureta[1]

5.1. FINANCIAL EDUCATION IS MORE EFFECTIVE THAN FINANCIAL INFORMATION

There is no doubt that investor protection is at the heart of the challenges facing financial industry today. As head of a bank that focuses its activity exclusively to wealth management and capital markets, Renta 4 Banco, and as President of the Spanish Institute of Financial Analysts, I consider these issues a top priority within my duties.

Sometimes we associate investor protection with mountains of complex information which, presumably, will give clarity on the financial assets offered to our clients and will avoid misunderstanding.

However, my experience, after working for and with investors during three decades, is that this complex information many times is even more misleading. A basic pedagogy, proper names for the assets, and an active role and engagement of the financial entities in the education of investors, telling them clearly that achieving a superior financial return without suffering volatility is, to say it bluntly, a dream.

I'll start sharing some strong convictions
- information plays a key role when it comes to protecting investors, but, by the very nature of what financial markets and financial investments are today, that role plays second best and what really is more effective is education, hence the financial education of investors. Financial education is powerful tool than information in order to protect investors;
- the responsibility for the education of investors has to be taken on by financial institutions as we are those in contact with them, know them and live their experiences and concerns;
- I firmly believe that those financial institutions that are capable of integrating within their business model the financial education of their clients will be the winners;

---

[1]   President of Renta 4 Banco and of Fundación de Estudios Financieros.

- the financial industry as a whole must take very seriously the challenge of financial education and pedagogy for investors in order to prevent and avoid a huge deception of retail investors if unconventional monetary policies don't have a happy end.

Personally I put these ideas into practice as much as I can.

As President of Renta 4 Banco, I take part in many meetings and seminars per year with clients, listening to them and conveying to them our views on investment alternatives, risks, expected returns on various assets, threats and opportunities that exist, how to diversify risk, and so on. I think that this competitive edge has provided growth at Renta 4 Banco for over almost three decades as well as has built a firm relationship with clients, a relationship that has grown stronger over the consecutive market crises. Proximity with our clients is our best marketing tool.

Based on this experience I will point out four issues:

5.2.   NAMES

Financial assets are not easy to understand but the first thing everybody hears is their names. And our industry has a long tradition of finding and creating attractive names, seductive names, for toxic products. Misleading names for bad products in order to get clients' money.

A good example is 'fixed income'. Even plain vanilla instruments, like a bond, or fixed income securities, contain complexities difficult to understand for ordinary citizens. I recall how in 1994 when the Fed raised interest rates in the US, an increase, which was translated into all fixed income markets round the world, caused great losses to fixed income funds. Investors could not grasp how they could lose money in an asset considered as 'fixed income'. Even so, some financial journalists inquired, amazed, how was it possible for fixed income products to drop in value and hence translated into losses just as interest rates were rising.

The misconception is that 'fixed income' does not necessarily mean 'fixed return'. If interest rates go up the bond which I purchased at a lower rate suddenly and rightly is worth less. If I sell before its maturity, I will cause myself a loss. The experience of 1994 inflicted considerable damage to the investment fund industry due to this episode.

Here we see something that is a common denominator in almost all problems or financial scandals I have known of, the use of a wrong name for a given product that is misleading for investors.

A wrong name for a product makes any information rendered useless. The complexity of financial assets means that although we hand over to investors all possible information on the product, in many cases such an ample flow of data is worthless since quite plainly it is not understood. Sometimes it is never read. This is what I call "explain all so that nothing is understood". Nothing is done in bad faith; it's just the way it is. To be honest with ourselves, sometimes a degree of bad faith can be found.

But everyone understands the name, and if we talk, as an example, about funds with 5% return, the common investor will understand that such given fund will return 5% irrespective of as many warnings as given by the fund.

Incidents associated with wrong names can be seen on multiple occasions where the product has caused problems to retail investors.

Preferred shares, deposits or structured bonds…all of these names sound quite well, the problem lies in that irrespective of how much information is given by them, the name is misleading.

Sometimes the problem goes beyond the fact that it creates confusion. Such was the case with the now famous 'convertible' bonds issued in Spain by several entities, which were later found to be compulsorily converted into shares. In this case the name is not only misleading but incorrect, inadequate since it does not reflect the reality of the asset. Again, the offering document clearly stated that the conversion was mandatory and at a pre-determined price. Nevertheless, the retail investor could only see that the bond would yield him a high interest. In all honesty, the truth is that at the time of marketing the bond and at the time of subscribing it, branch managers played down the risk related to the product. Needless to say that the hidden risks became a reality.

Another example of a misleading name is the dot com companies in the late nineties. They were called 'new economy companies' and 'fast growing companies'. It sounds really fascinating: who is not going to invest in it? Unfortunately, the reality was quite different.

Another example was the so called 'structured bonds' and 'structured deposits'. They were sold as safe deposits or safe bonds but they had complex options inside.

In Spain we had the so called 'preference shares'. The name was completely misleading because the reality was that these shares were subordinated debt.

Compulsory convertible bonds has been another bad experience for the investors. These bonds were sold like 'convertibles', but they had to be 'converted' obligatory at a fixed price and the problem was that this price was quite high. Again a misleading name.

To put it bluntly, sometimes the devil is hidden in the name hence all attention must be paid to it.

5.3.   ZIRP ENVIRONMENT BRINGS SERIOUS RISKS

The need for proper financial education is crucial in an environment of zero interest rate policy (ZIRP), which in turn pushes investors to buy risk in search for higher returns.

The ZIRP environment – and the risks for investors, the search for yield means troubles ahead. Experience says that, although more necessary than ever, it is very difficult to have a sensible speech when everybody wants to dance.

To make my point clear: it may not be very commercial to advise clients that certain assets involve risks or that they have to confront 1% returns if they do not want to assume risk.

Martin Feldstein and Robert Rubin, in *Wall Street Journal* (13 August 2014) commented on this problem. They said that the Fed is relying on macroprudential policy to avoid systemic risk arising from the ZIRP and QE (Quantitative Easing) programs. They say this will be ok in order to make banks more resilient, but systemic risks extended to a number of other institutions and asset managers and there the issues around macroprudential regulation become much more complicated.

And I would add, a systemic risk extends to retail investors as a consequence.

"There are many potential examples of heightened risks. For one, if hedge funds hold excessively priced assets that at some point start to adjust, there could be a contagion and snowball effect, especially given the crowded trades that hedge funds make. That could affect broader markets.

The yields spreads of low quality bonds have fallen dramatically, the S&P is near record highs, volatility is very low, and the Spanish 10 year bond, for example, is trading at its lowest rate since 1789. The buyers of these instruments include insurance companies and individuals. In the short run markets tend to be psychological and in the longer run tend to reflect fundamentals. Whether and how much markets are mispriced relative to fundamentals is always uncertain. But when markets have moved across the board as much as they now have, that should signal a warning of excesses".

The conclusion of Martin Feldstein and Robert Rubin is that policy makers, and I add, all of us, should have a realistic view of the broad range of existing systemic risks and of the limits of the government's macroprudential tools.

In my opinion this is another reason and attaches a greater role to the financial industry in the responsibility to educate investors. I would say, allow me the audacity, the boldness to be a little bit daring, that financial education is the most powerful tool in hands of the policy makers and of the financial industry as a whole, to address properly the huge challenges that the growing role of financial markets and the deleveraging process pose to (economic and financial stability) all of us.

We can see some examples of risky assets because of ZIRP:

- High yields. With zero interest rates in the safest assets, investors buy high yield assets. Risk premiums have shrunk enormously, and do not reflect the real risks. In bonds there is a risk not only of default but also of illiquidity, as we saw in the autumn 2008.

- Cocos (Contingent Convertible Securities) – a new toxic asset? Although – it is true that the product was only sold to qualified investors and institutions, at the end it is the retail investor, the one who buys the pension fund or investment fund that originally bought the product. In this case the problem is not in the name, since in this case the name is very protective and warns of the risks. The problem is that the Coco is bundled in a fund or in a technical insurance reserve or in an asset that is then sold to retail investors. Which are the problems with Cocos? The great John Dizard described them in an article last August 1 in the *Financial Times* entitled "Coconuts: the return of toxic-bubble era stuff".
  He said: "There is a boom in issuance of European banks' 'additional tier one capital', which last year we would have called 'cocos' or contingent convertible securities. Up until June, there had been €28 bn raised by European banks. These are among the most opaque debt securities in the known world. They can have coupon payments suspended or be subject to mandatory conversion to equity or complete writedowns, all at the discretion of the issuing bank or its regulators, even while the bank is still paying dividends on its common stock. This sounds like toxic bubble-era stuff, but in the first part of this year the capital-markets desks selling AT1s have had buyside customers complaining they cannot get enough of each issue. Simple enough: the AT1s are the highest-yielding securities to be found that pass the test of your compliance officer or lawyers. Recent issues by Barclays and Deutsche can give you a touch under 7 per cent, which is enough to meet or exceed benchmark returns in this QE-scarred world. At the junk end of the market, AT1 paper from peripheral issuers can yield over 9 per cent. On top of that, there have been significant capital gains from AT1s this year, with spreads on southern European banks coming in by around a third. It is true that if you read all the way through the offering

documents, the European banks make it clear that you may not be getting those yields and capital gains forever. These days, though, many investors believe next year and maybe the year after would be good enough. I believe the text is quite clear.

- ETFs (Exchange Traded Funds). The huge success of ETFs is causing several risks to investor protection. The first one is that not all ETFs are clear. The so called 'synthetic' ETFs and other confusing names (active managed ETF for example, a contradiction in itself, reverse, etc...) create risks in understanding what one is effectively investing in. Another example is the risk, which has taken place, during the market sessions of the 15 and 16 of October. ETFs amplify market volatility by generating simultaneous movements of millions of retail investors in the same direction, and these usually guided by media coverage (news, break of technical levels,...) caused a 'stampede' effect. This is an issue to watch, no doubt.

- Another present and arguable example (not deceiving but misleading information) is the SCRIP DIVIDEND (where shareholders receive shares instead of cash dividend). Shareholders should have a better understanding of the financial implications of such a dividend policy and not just misleading information on tax benefits. Shareholders are paid a dividend which is a liability against another liability. At the end they are paid with something that belongs to them, not to the company which pays it. They pay them with a liability versus another liability. We should at least make a difference (and in this case we talk about information) when we publish the dividend yield of listed companies also, at the time of comparing which company pays the highest dividend, the difference between a cash dividend, the purest of them all, and a dividend paid in new shares, which is not the same. The latter must be explained to investors.

- MAB markets for growing companies (Spanish markets for alternative investments) investing in less solid companies can leave the investor with a sour experience. But even in continuous market surprises can also be negative. The idea is: if investors know that MAB is a market for companies do not need to fulfill the same requirements as those listed on the Continuous Market, and therefore investment in them leads to higher levels of risk, we have already gone a long way. It is certainly true that information could be improved and bettering it would help, and it is true that rules that imply that companies with a given market capitalization should be transferred to the Continuous Market, are of help, but the basic principle is that retail investors must be aware that placing a significant amount of their savings in MAB companies is not a good idea, if they do not wish to take excessive risk in their investments. The same thing is true for some companies of the continuous market and financial entities should advise their clients about it in an active manner.

One good thing about shares is that everyone knows they imply risk. The same culture does not apply to bonds. We must convey the culture that bonds can also inflict a loss that is the reality.

Most of these examples have one thing in common, to think there can be big returns without risk, like 'Eldorado'.

5.4.   A PRACTICAL WAY TO EDUCATE INVESTORS: TO TELL THEM A SIMPLE IDEA LIKE ELDORADO DOES NOT EXIST. THERE IS NO PHILOSOPHICAL STONE

The basic challenge is how to provide normalized products and services in markets which are volatile in nature to an investor who is looking for his own Eldorado. The first step is to try and change his perception. Convince him that he has to forget about the next big thing, Eldorado.

But the problem is that this approach is not too commercial except in times of a crisis.

The ZIRP environment and the risks for investors, the search for yield means headache ahead. But it is very difficult to have a sensible speech when everybody wants to dance. Again, the problem for the industry to educate investors is that it may not be too 'commercial' to tell clients that certain positions involve risks or tell them they have to be happy with a 1% return if they do not want to assume risks.

Today we have to tell investors that yields will be structurally lower for all the categories of assets, and more return means more risk. It is not an easy message. It is an 'uncomfortable truth'

5.5.   A VERY SERIOUS PROBLEM: HOW TO PROTECT RETAIL INVESTORS FROM 'BLACK SWANS'?

This problem connects with investor protection against events or risks of low probability (for them really to happen) but of high consequences. The protection against market crashes, against 'black swans'. By their structure, I would say that by their very nature, financial markets are not designed or prepared to deal with such events. Not even the financial industry. It is true that progress has been made to expand the capital base of financial institutions so that they are able to absorb losses on their balance sheets from events as the above mentioned without there being systemic risk for financial or economic stability. But let's not talk about that. We talk about how to protect investors against a sudden loss in the value of their financial assets unexpected and very large, 30% to 80%, derived from a market crash.

Overall my experience is that no one manages third party assets taking into account such events as an essential investment strategy. Quite simply the industry believes that if these take place they will affect all players and the only rule that counts is: our company should be less hit than the rest or at least less than the average. It is also thought, not without reason, that to manage assets on the basis of a future market crash is more or less impossible since it would lead to a paralysis, inaction and like in the Gospel not knowing how to place talent in the right spot.

And yet it is a key issue when it comes to protecting investors especially retail investors, because it is well known that the retail investor tends to arrive 'late' to be a 'follower' and invest in assets when they are overbought.

In today's markets, as of today, this protection is, in my opinion more important than ever because the ZIRP is prompting investors to take higher levels of risk and if a market crush occurs the consequences for investor confidence will be more devastating than ever.

If the goal is to make the financial system safe for the small investors, Governments should look at their own policies promoting risks.

How to protect the investor against black swans? Again, information here is a very limited tool and yet education is much more effective. A culture of risk-awareness, a real diversification policy, prudence, are the only ones that can save us, or at least partially, from these black swans.

Another two key points are to avoid leverage and to foster diversification.

These are simple things, it is not even 'financial education' it is only 'basic pedagogy' but with this you avoid 80% of the problems

5.6. TO INTEGRATE INVESTOR EDUCATION IN ONE'S BUSINESS MODEL IS PROFITABLE. FOR THE INDUSTRY AS A WHOLE IT IS A NECESSITY

We have to vindicate the best of what the industry was a few decades ago, before all the big bangs. Back to basics. Plain language with investors.

Don't get me wrong. I am a believer in financial innovation as I am a believer in technology and innovation. But we are not talking about that, we are talking about ordinary people and about serving ordinary people. About people. And other rules play here. Is another thing. More boring, more routinaire, but less toxic.

I will conclude. I am convinced that being a 'good player' and playing our role with a concept of 'construction' and a concept building things to last is far more profitable than doing short term marketing based on false promises.

And investors' education is a powerful tool in that long term marketing strategy and business strategy, being at the same time more necessary than ever in today and future markets, in which financial assets will gain share in the pocket of families precisely when the financial industry needs to create margin more than in any previous period, and in which the so called systemic risks are there, even if they are hidden or they are dispersed among millions of retail investors instead of being concentrated in the banks' balance sheets.

So I am firmly convinced that integrating financial education into business models should be a priority for financial institutions and the financial industry as a whole.

6. THE ROLE OF BANKS IN FOSTERING FINANCIAL INCLUSION

José Manuel González-Páramo[1]

6.1. INTRODUCTION

The lack of financial abilities is considered to be one of the most important problems in modern societies. These societies have increasing levels of indebtedness and saving needs, with individuals who do not have a comprehensive understanding of basic financial issues. Financial literacy has been found to be very low around the world, irrespective of the level of financial market development (Lusardi and Mitchell, 2011a).

Global trends anticipate that the relationship between individuals and financial systems is going to intensify. Factors such as increased life expectancy and the changes in the welfare state's coverage mean that, increasingly, individuals have to be involved in financial decisions. Decisions such as saving for retirement, expenditure on education and health, or buying a home, are taken in a scenario in which financial markets are more accessible to consumers, due to major technological progress (reducing transaction costs between supply and demand) and the appearance of new – and more complex – financial services. Although this progress is positive, it increases the responsibility for saving, debt, investment and asset decumulation through tailored financial contracts.

The combination of more complex financial products and insufficient financial capability has been argued to be one of the causes behind the real estate boom in the United States and the consequent subprime mortgage crisis, which expanded into a global financial crisis. Following the crisis, international organisations, governments and private institutions have included financial education in their agendas, evidencing the increasing relevance of financial literacy (Volpe and Mumaw, 2010). In 2012, the OECD included, for the first time, financial literacy questions in its PISA assessment of 15 year-old students, being the first large-scale international study to assess the financial literacy of young people. Young people are an especially interesting target for financial literacy, since they need to be prepared for dealing with increasingly complex financial decisions in the future.

In emerging markets, access to basic financial products for low-income individuals is growing much faster than the financial capability of these segments of the population. Deb and Kubzansky (2012) estimate that between 370 million

---

[1]   Member of the Board of Directors and Chief Officer, Global Economics, Regulation and Public Affairs, BBVA.

and 690 million low-income earners worldwide now have access to formal or quasi-formal financial services, but have not received any form of financial education.

This paper aims to discuss the role of financial service providers, and particularly commercial banks, in promoting financial literacy. Traditionally, the involvement of those firms in financial education projects has been considered as a corporate social responsibility (CSR) activity towards the communities where they operate. This paper explores the incipient research on the economic impact of financial literacy to see whether there is a business case, apart from CSR, for the banks to invest in financial education programmes.

The paper is structured as follows. Section 2 defines financial literacy and the close concept of financial capability. Section 3 analyses the economic case for the banks' involvement in fostering financial education. Finally, Section 4 concludes with some considerations that should be taken into account to properly address the financial literacy challenge.

6.2. THE CONCEPT OF FINANCIAL LITERACY

Financial literacy is defined as people's ability to process economic information and make informed decisions about financial planning, wealth accumulation, indebtedness and pensions. The OECD gives a more complete definition of financial literacy: "the process by which financial consumers/investors improve their understanding of products, concepts and financial risks and, via information, instruction and objective advice, develop the skills and confidence to be more aware of financial risks and opportunities, take well-founded decisions, know where to go for help and carry out other effective interventions to improve their financial position" (OECD, 2005).

Financial literacy includes the ability to discriminate between different financial alternatives, speak clearly on financial matters and save for the future. According to these and other definitions, financial literacy is an important ingredient in increasing financial capability and thus affecting economic behaviour (Lyons *et al.*, 2006; Mandell, 2006; and Hilgert *et al.*, 2003).

Some authors establish a clear difference between the knowledge-based concept of financial literacy and the broader concept of financial capability, defined as "the internal capacity to act in one's best financial interest, given socioeconomic and environmental conditions" (Perotti *et al.*, 2013). This approach is based on the principle that knowledge is an important, but not always sufficient, input to behavioural change, and that the outcome of relevance is how individuals behave in relation to financial products rather than what they know about them. Johnson and Sherraden (2007) point out that financial capability requires access to the appropriate financial institutions and products, and not just the acquisition of knowledge and the development of skills.

It has been argued that financial capacities, responsible to a large degree for financial behaviour, are determined by different elements which can be separated into two groups: cognitive factors (knowledge, understanding or acumen, among others) and non-cognitive (personal attitudes). The cognitive aspects are considered to be part of the acquired financial literacy that can improve using different practices relating to financial education and learning by experience.

6.3. THE ECONOMIC CASE FOR BANKS' INVOLVEMENT IN FINANCIAL EDUCATION

Most of the research on the economic impact of financial literacy has focused on the private benefits for individuals, arising from behavioural changes related to lifetime financial planning, better money management and signing up for better financial products. As those changes in consumers' behaviour affect the financial service providers, there are a number of direct and indirect channels through which financial literacy has the potential to be beneficial for banks and other financial institutions. Those channels are: i) increasing demand from both previously unbanked segments and existing customers, ii) reducing credit risk, and iii) enhancing the soundness and efficiency of the financial system.

Financial illiteracy has been identified in the literature as one of the barriers to achieving a more inclusive financial environment. Indeed, some definitions of financial inclusion consider financial capability as one of its key ingredients, together with access and engagement with the financial system (Deb and Kubzansky, 2012).

The strong relation between financial literacy/capability and financial inclusion has been also highlighted by the World Bank: "In order to foster participation in financial markets, consumers need to be better informed about the features of financial products, have the confidence to interact with providers of financial services, know how to choose and use these products and where to seek advice, and be aware of their rights and available redress mechanisms" (Perotti *et al.*, 2013).

Financial literacy has therefore the potential to increase demand for financial products from previously unbanked segments of the population. As an example, in the developed world, where the conditions are highly inclusive, 24% of people have a mortgage, compared to only 3% in the developing, un-inclusive world (Demirgüç-Kunt and Klapper, 2013). More generally, financial participation aids progress and development of the financial sector, something inextricably linked to economic growth (Perotti *et al.*, 2013). As credit becomes more widely available, as a result of the development of capital markets, SMEs have the opportunity to grow, therefore creating more jobs and potentially more financial intermediation.

Moreover, as adults with higher levels of financial education are more likely to plan and save for retirement and accumulate more wealth (Bernheim *et al.*, 2001; Cole *et al.*, 2011; Lusardi, 2009; Lusardi and Mitchell, 2011b), financial literacy has the potential to increase the demand for savings products not just from unbanked individuals but also from existing customers. Besides, financial literacy could help to retain existing customers as there is some evidence of financial education strengthening consumers' relationships with banks (Burhouse *et al.*, 2007).

On the other hand, financial literacy has been found to have a positive impact on customers' debt management and has therefore the potential to reduce the credit risk faced by banks. Lusardi and Tufano (2009) show that individuals with low levels of financial literacy are more likely to get into high-cost debt agreements and suffer indebtedness problems. Conversely, some financial training programmes have been shown to be linked to a decrease in arrears, an improvement in repayment rates or, more generally, to a better performance of borrowers' businesses (McIntosh *et al.*, 2006; Drexler *et al.*, 2014; Karlan and Valdivia, 2011).

Deb and Kubzansky (2012) point to 'induction training' and 'delinquency management' as cost-effective initiatives for banks and microfinance institutions (MFIs) since they have the potential to improve credit performance. Induction training – already a requirement by most MFIs – is completed before the loan agreement is signed, laying out its features and expectations. This process removes any confusion concerning the loan, reduces late payments and defaults and generates greater revenues for the financial institution.

Delinquency training represents a shift to a more expensive, but more focused, teaching model. Here, customers deemed to be in risk of default or who have poorly performing loans are invited for classes, camouflaged as other events and often laden with incentives. Although these classes are quite expensive to the providers, around $14 per person, empirical evidence reveals that the banks often make up that amount due to the reduced frequency of defaults.

At the aggregate level, financial literacy may contribute to preserve the stability and soundness of the financial system as a whole. One of the reasons for this is the previously discussed improvement in customers' creditworthiness and the resultant reduction in subprime lending. In addition, financially literate consumers are likely to exert stronger market discipline on banks, leading to more prudent management practices, and to react to market conditions in more predictable ways (OECD, 2013; Widdowson and Hailwood, 2007).

In addition, financial literacy has been argued to enhance the efficiency of the financial sector. Empirical evidence reveals that individuals with higher levels of financial knowledge sign up for less costly mortgages in terms of both interest rates and additional fees (Gerardi *et al.*, 2010; Lusardi and Tufano, 2009; Moore, 2003). This means that more financially capable consumers are able to search for and compare financial products and services more effectively, promoting innovation and competition between providers (Widdowson and Hailwood, 2007). In contrast, insufficient levels of financial literacy, together with complex products and disclosures, erode competition in the financial sector and therefore efficiency.

The stability, soundness and efficiency of the financial system will result in a reduced need for costly regulation, supervision or government aid (OECD, 2013). As a result, banks will enjoy higher levels of autonomy, lower compliance costs and regulatory distortions, more societal tolerance for their intermediation and better reputations.

6.4.   CONCLUDING REMARKS

As is well known in the literature, market failures make it difficult for people and families to develop financial capabilities and knowledge by themselves in order to interact with the financial system in more equitable conditions. This pervasive market failure, together with the social benefits of financial literacy, makes the case for governmental intervention in encouraging financial education. However, beyond this, banks also have enormous incentives for contributing to financial education, apart from corporate social responsibility. As we discussed in the previous section, they may benefit directly from higher demand and lower credit risk and, more generally, from preserving the soundness of the financial system and enhancing its efficiency.

To address the financial literacy challenge in the most efficient way, it is important to study the impact of different educational programmes and carefully consider their implementation. Nowadays, most of the financial educational initiatives are one-off, group-based classes and only provide short-term training with no follow-up. This is particularly problematic as participants in the programmes show that without repetition of the contents, retention is considerably lower and is quickly forgotten (Deb and Kubzansky, 2012).

In addition, more often than not, individuals exhibit change in financial behaviour only in the short term. This is due to a 'one size fits all' approach that typically provides general information rather than a customised, focused approach intended to achieve a specific change in financial behaviour according to the individual's needs. In this respect, facilitating change in financial behaviour has proven to be much more common when educational programmes are implemented at the appropriate moment; a time "when people may be especially motivated to gain and use financial knowledge and skills and are able to put this knowledge to work" (Perotti *et al.*, 2013). This highlights the potential role of banks in delivering financial educational as they get in touch with individuals at the very time when they are facing financial decisions.

On the other hand, financial educational efforts should be targeted at the demographic groups that have the greatest needs, such as women and children. The former have a longer life expectancy and are therefore more likely to experience a 'financial hardship'. The latter are likely to face more complex financial markets at the age at which they must make independent financial decisions, requiring increased financial capability.

Since traditional financial educational programmes are too expensive to be cost-effective (Deb and Kubzansky, 2012), there is a need to innovate in the delivery channels of financial education. Banks and other financial institutions could provide training to their customers, using the same new technological channels that are being developed to distribute products and services. Just as this may lower banks' distributional costs, it has also the potential to reduce the delivery cost of financial education.

Finally, given the relevance of financial literacy for the economic well-being of modern societies, a unified strategy should be adopted, bringing together the public and the private sector. Banks are called to play an important role in this financial literacy challenge. It is not just a moral responsibility towards the societies where they operate, but also a consistent investment in their business sustainability.

REFERENCES

BERNHEIM, D., GARRETT, D. & MAKI, D., 2001, "Education and saving: The long-term effects of high school financial curriculum mandates", *Journal of Public Economics*, 80(3), 435-565.

BURHOUSE, S., HARRIS, A. & REYNOLDS, L., 2007, "Banking on Financial Education", *FDIC Quarterly*, 1(2), 33-42.

COLE, S., SAMPSON, T. & ZIA, B., 2011, "Prices or Knowledge? What Drives Demand for Financial Services in Emerging Markets?", *Journal of Finance*, 66(6), 1933-67.

DEB, A. & KUBZANSKY, M., 2012, *Bridging the Gap: The Business Case for Financial Capability. A report commissioned and funded by the Citi Foundation*, Cambridge, Mass. Monitor, March.

DEMIRGÜÇ-KUNT, A., & KLAPPER, L., 2013, "Measuring Financial Inclusion: Explaining Variation in Use of Financial Services across and within Countries", *Brookings Papers on Economic Activity*, (1), 279-340.

DREXLER, A., FISCHER, G. & SCHOAR, A., 2014, "Keeping it simple: Financial literacy and rules of thumb", *American Economic Journal: Applied Economics*, 6(2), 1-31.

GERARDI, K., GOETTE, L. & MEIER, S., 2010, "Financial literacy and subprime mortgage delinquency: Evidence from a survey matched to administrative data", *Federal Reserve Bank of Atlanta Working Paper Series*, No. 2010-10.

HILGERT, M.A., HOGARTH, J.M. & BEVERLY, S.G., 2003, "Household financial management: The connection between knowledge and behavior", *Federal Reserve Bulletin*, 89 (7), 309-322.

JOHNSON, E. & SHERRADEN, M.S., 2007, "From financial literacy to financial capability among youth", *Journal of Sociology and Social Welfare*, 34 (3), 119-145.

KARLAN, D. & VALDIVIA, M., 2011,. "Teaching entrepreneurship: Impact of business training on microfinance clients and institutions", *Review of Economics and Statistics*, 93(2), 510-527.

LUSARDI, A., 2009, "U.S. Household Savings Behavior: The Role of Financial Literacy, Information and Financial Education Programs" in C. FOOTE, L. GOETTE and S. MEIER (eds.), *Policymaking Insights from Behavioral Economics*, Federal Reserve Bank of Boston, pp. 109-149.

LUSARDI, A. & MITCHELL, O., 2011a, "Financial literacy around the world: an overview", *Journal of Pensions Economics and Finance*, 10(4), 497-508.

LUSARDI, A. & MITCHELL, O., 2011b, "Financial literacy and planning: implications for retirement wellbeing", *NBER Working Paper*, No. 17078, Cambridge, MA, National Bureau of Economic Research.

LUSARDI, A. & TUFANO, P., 2009, "Debt Literacy, Financial Experiences, and Overindebtedness", *NBER Working Paper*, No. 14808, Cambridge, MA, National Bureau of Economic Research.

LYONS, A.C., PALMER, L., JAYARATNE, K.S. & SCHERPF, E., 2006, "Are we making the grade? A national overview of financial education and program evaluation", *Journal of Consumer Affairs*, 40 (2), 208-235.

MANDELL, L., 2006, "Financial literacy: If it's so important, why isn't it improving?", *Networks Financial Institute Policy Brief 2006-PB*, 8.

MCINTOSH, C., SADOULET, E. & DE JANVRY, A., 2006, *Better Lending and Better Clients: Credit Bureau Impact on Microfinance*, BASIS, Madison, WI Brief, 45.

MOORE, D., 2003, "Survey of Financial Literacy in Washington State: Knowledge, Behavior, Attitudes, and Experiences", *Social and Economic Sciences Research Center Technical Report* 03-39, Washington State University.

OCDE, 2005, "Improving Financial Literacy: Analysis of Issues and Policies", *Financial Market Trends*, OECD Publishing, Vol. 2, 111-123, OCDE, Paris.

OECD (2013), *PISA 2012 assessment and analytical framework: mathematics, reading, science, problem solving and financial literacy*, OECD Publishing.

PEROTTI, V., ZOTTEL, S., IAROSSI, G. & BOLAJI-ADIO, A., 2013, *Making sense of financial capability surveys around the World: a review of existing financial capability and literacy measurement instruments*, Washington DC, World Bank.

VOLPE, R. & MUMAW, K., 2010, "Financial Literacy and the Subprime Mortgage Crisis", *Journal of Business and Accounting*, 2(1), 17-31.

WIDDOWSON, D. & HAILWOOD, K., 2007, "Financial literacy and its role in promoting a sound financial system", *Reserve Bank of New Zealand Bulletin*, 70(2).

7. THE ROLE OF REGULATORS IN INVESTOR EDUCATION

Lori J. Schock[1]

7.1. INTRODUCTION[2]

While Congress created the U.S. Securities and Exchange Commission in 1934, it wasn't until the mid-1990s that the Commission began to focus in earnest on investor education. The SEC stands as the primary regulator of securities and financial professionals in the United States. For over 20 years, the SEC's Office of Investor Education and Advocacy has sought to support the SEC's investor protection mission by helping U.S. investors obtain the fundamental information they need to make informed investment decisions and avoid securities fraud.

OIEA administers the SEC's nationwide investor education program. We provide a variety of services and tools to address the problems and questions that individual investors may face. OIEA conducts educational outreach; assists with investor complaints and inquiries; and facilitates individual investors in bringing their perspectives to the Commission and its staff.

7.2. SEC INVESTOR OUTREACH AND EDUCATION PROGRAMS

In addition to participation in financial literacy and investor education programs across the United States and throughout the year, we also develop and maintain the SEC's Investor.gov website, publish Investor Alerts and Bulletins, and partner with outside organizations to help investors better understand how they can protect themselves when they make their investment decisions.

Investor.gov

In October 2009, the SEC launched Investor.gov, its first-ever website focused exclusively on investor education. This website aims to help investors educate themselves on issues affecting their investment decisions and includes information

---

[1]   Director, Office of Investor Education and Advocacy, U.S. Securities and Exchange Commission.
[2]   *Required disclaimer: The Securities and Exchange Commission, as a matter of policy, disclaims responsibility for any private publication or statement by any of its employees. The views expressed in this presentation do not necessarily reflect the views of the SEC, its Commissioners, or other members of the SEC's staff.*

such as how to detect fraud. Individual investors who access this website can learn information on a variety of investing topics, including how to research investments and investment professionals, understand fees, and detect fraud. The content is designed to be easily understandable, including the 'Investing Basics' section, which explains common retail investment products in plain language.

Investor.gov also offers tools and materials targeted to investors who may face particular investment needs, such as members of the military, teachers, and retirees. In addition, we work with the Department of Treasury to ensure that key resources from Investor.gov are included in relevant sections of the Financial Literacy and Education Commission's financial education website, MyMoney.gov.

Print Publications

For those investors who prefer print publications, we continue to offer these materials to help individuals make informed investment choices and detect fraud. We emphasize factors and important questions for investors to consider and ask before they invest. All of our materials are available free of charge and not copyrighted, so that the widest possible dissemination is encouraged. Our most popular brochures are offered in both English and Spanish, including publications focused on mutual funds and variable annuities. The SEC's Saving and Investing for Students booklet explains different types of financial products, the realities of risk, and other key information students need to know in setting their financial goals. Individuals can order free copies of any SEC print publication by visiting Investor.gov. Individuals can also receive SEC brochures by requesting the Financial Literacy and Education Commission's MyMoney toolkit. Additionally, we have developed a series of information sheets including such topics as Asset Allocation, Target Date Funds, Ponzi Schemes and Affinity Fraud.

7.3.   INVESTOR ALERTS AND BULLETINS

Another way the SEC reaches out to individual investors is through our Investor Alerts and Bulletins. Investor Alerts and Bulletins are short articles written to inform the investing public about particular topics. Investor Bulletins provide individual investors with important information regarding various investment-related topics. Investor Alerts warn investors about potentially questionable activity that the Commission's staff has been made aware of, including through investor complaints and inquiries. In the past year we published a record number of twenty-eight different Investor Alerts and Bulletins warning investors of possible fraudulent schemes, including affinity fraud and schemes involving virtual currencies, and educating them on investment-related matters.

OIEA publishes Investor Alerts and Bulletins on the SEC's website, SEC.gov, as well as on Investor.gov. We also disseminate them through a variety of other channels including a designated RSS feed, Gov.delivery, press releases, Facebook and our Twitter account, @SEC_Investor_Ed. At the end of 2014, we had over 45,000 followers. We continue to explore the possible utilization of other digital media tools to reach more individual investors with limited additional cost.

7.4.   REACHING INVESTORS THROUGH PARTNERSHIPS – RECENT EXAMPLES

As part of its mission of investor protection, the SEC encourages investment literacy for all Americans. Our partnerships with other government agencies, localities and private sector financial education are vital to helping us reach investors within our limited resources.

Some recent examples of our partnerships to reach investors include:

1.   Outsmarting Investment Fraud. We continue to work with FINRA, AARP and state securities regulators on a campaign designed to reduce investment fraud among older Americans. The campaign is based on research funded by the FINRA Investor Education Foundation. With our partners, we regularly participate in events that teach seniors how to identify common persuasion techniques used by con artists. We also train attendees on how to 'ask and check' about investments and investment professionals before they invest so they can protect themselves and teach others in their community about effective fraud detection techniques.

2.   Internal Revenue Service (IRS) Tax Refund Check Mailings. Over the last few years, we have worked with the Financial Management Service at the IRS to communicate messages on saving and investing to Americans across the country. During the month of April, approximately eight million individuals will receive IRS tax refund mailings that contain an insert promoting investor education resources from the SEC through Investor.gov.

3.   Financial Literacy and Education Commission. The SEC is a member of the Financial Literacy and Education Commission ('FLEC'). The Financial Literacy and Education Commission was established under the Fair and Accurate Credit Transactions Act of 2003. The FLEC was tasked to develop a national financial education web site (MyMoney.gov) along with a hotline (1-888-My Money) and a national strategy on financial education. It is

chaired by the Secretary of the Treasury and made up of the heads of more than twenty additional federal agencies. In addition to the activities noted above, the SEC serves on FLEC's Research and Evaluation Subcommittee.

4. SEC-Academy of Finance Shadowing Program. Consistent with Section 342 of the Dodd-Frank Act, the SEC has developed an SEC Shadowing Program with the Academy of Finance representing students from inner city high schools in the DC region. The Academy of Finance connects high school students with an interest in finance with the world of financial services.

5. Other Partnerships. The SEC is a partner and ex officio board member of the Jump$tart Coalition for Financial Literacy, a mission partner of the American Savings Education Council, a charter member of the Department of Defense's Financial Readiness Initiative, and a founding advisor of the Alliance for Investor Education. We participate in numerous local and national financial literacy events each year including Military Saves Week, America Saves Week, and Financial Literacy Day on Capitol Hill.

7.5.   SEC INVESTOR ASSISTANCE PROGRAM

OIEA's Office of Investor Assistance responds to questions, complaints, and suggestions from members of the public. The Office handles investment-related complaints and questions from tens of thousands of individual investors and others every year. Investors contact us seeking information about the securities markets, securities laws and regulations, investment products, and financial professionals. Investors also submit complaints involving brokers, investment advisers, transfer agents, mutual funds and other companies that issue securities.

OIEA staff directly answers the majority of the contacts, after consultation with expert staff within the agency when necessary. They also forward investor complaints that involve potential violations of the federal securities laws or potential harm to investors to the agency's Tips, Complaints and Referrals (TCR) system for triage by the Division of Enforcement's Office of Market Intelligence, and forward investor complaints involving a regulated entity (broker-dealer, investment adviser, or transfer agent) to the entity for a response addressing the investor's concerns. OIEA also regularly handles correspondence referred by the Chairman's Office, Congressional offices and the White House.

7.6. INVESTOR TESTING AND DODD-FRANK STUDIES

7.6.1. Disclosure Document Evaluation Study Dodd-Frank Act Section 917

The SEC conducted investor testing as part of its Disclosure Document Evaluation Study (the 'Study'). The purpose of this investor testing was to examine the effectiveness of SEC-mandated disclosure documents, specifically, the Form 10-K annual report and the mutual fund shareholder report, in communicating useful information to individual investors. The Study was designed to gather feedback from investors in order to determine how these disclosure materials could more effectively communicate information to individual investors. The Study entailed:

– obtaining investors' evaluation of the Form 10-K and the mutual fund shareholder report, including a baseline assessment against which to measure future disclosures;
– identifying specific areas of these documents where investors think current disclosure is adequate;
– identifying specific areas of these documents that could be improved;
– suggesting new document formats as alternative ways to express or summarize complex financial information in both hard copy and digital formats; and
– proposing actions and/or solutions to simplify documents for use by the individual investor.

In examining these disclosures, OIEA worked with the SEC's Division of Corporation Finance to evaluate investors' responses to current Form 10-K materials, and with the SEC's Division of Investment Management to evaluate investors' responses to current mutual fund shareholder reports. These evaluations were designed to prioritize the importance and usefulness of each of the disclosure items within the Form 10-K and the mutual fund shareholder report, including information that is less useful and information that might be included in a revised document. The Study is responsive to the SEC's 2010-2015 Strategic Plan, which calls for investors to have access to disclosure documents that are useful for investment decision-making and for those materials to be provided in concise, easy-to-use formats.

The Study also served as a predicate for significant portions of a separate study regarding financial literacy among investors, as mandated by Section 917 of the Dodd-Frank Act. That provision called for the SEC to identify the existing level of financial literacy among retail investors; methods to improve the timing, content, and format of disclosures to investors with respect to financial intermediaries, investment products, and investment services; methods to increase the transparency of expenses and conflicts of interest in transactions involving investment services and products; and the most effective existing private and public efforts to educate investors. We delivered our final report to Congress in August 2012.

7.6.2. Dodd-Frank Act Section 919B

Section 919B of the Dodd-Frank Act directed the SEC to complete a study, including recommendations, of ways to improve the access of investors to registration information about registered and previously registered investment advisers, associated persons of investment advisers, brokers and dealers and their associated persons, and to identify additional information that should be made publicly available. The Act specified that the study include an analysis of the advantages and disadvantages of further centralizing access to registration information, and identify data pertinent to investors and method and format for displaying and publishing the data to enhance the information's accessibility and utility to investors.

OIEA prepared the study in consultation with the SEC's Division of Investment Management, the Division of Trading and Markets, the Division of Risk, Strategy, and Financial Innovation, and the Office of the General Counsel. OIEA also sought input from FINRA and state securities regulators.

The study made the following recommendations which have since been implemented:
1. unify FINRA's BrokerCheck and the SEC's Investment Adviser Public Disclosure ('IAPD') database search results;
2. add a ZIP code search function to BrokerCheck and IAPD;
3. add educational content to BrokerCheck and IAPD.

7.7. CONCLUSION

Improving financial literacy is an important goal that can empower individual investors to participate in the financial markets. By making it possible for investors to access educational materials that are understandable and geared to their interests and concerns, regulators can play a valuable role in assisting them to invest intelligently and to detect fraud. The SEC is committed to this important role in our rapidly changing markets.

8.   THE RISK OF RISK COMMITTEES[1]

Colin Mayer[2]

8.1.   WHAT SHOULD WE DO ABOUT FAILING FINANCIAL INSTITUTIONS?

At the end of 2014, in response to the Forex scandal it was announced that banks were to be subject to fines of $4.3bn[3]. Forex is destined to dwarf Libor where fines amounted to more than $6bn.

We have become immune to such revelations and almost take it for granted now that banks manipulate markets as in Forex and Libor, sell their customers wrong or mispriced products as in payments protection and interest rate hedges for small and medium sized companies, and take risks that threaten the viability of their institutions, as in the financial crisis.

Two of the largest and most important markets in the financial system have been systematically manipulated and regulators failed to identify evidence of this in pricing patterns. If they cannot do so in the largest markets then the chances are that other financial markets have been manipulated in one form or another without anyone noticing.

What should we do about it? We can impose ever-increasing fines on banks that are proven guilty. The evidence on this is that the impact of massive fines where they relate to the market as a whole (as in the Forex and Libor scandals) is modest[4]. The share price reactions of banks subject to such fines, even where investigations are unanticipated in advance by the market, are either insignificant or positive as banks are revealed to have furthered the interests of their shareholders at the expense of third parties.

The main response to the failures of financial institutions during the financial crisis and in the market rigging cases has been to require them to have risk committees, chief risk officers and to make the boards of banks responsible for monitoring and controlling risks. Is this the right approach?

---

[1]   This is a copy of the talk that Colin Mayer gave at the SUERF / CNMV Conference on "Challenges in Securities Market Regulation: Investor Protection and Corporate Governance" at the National Council for Scientific Research in Madrid on 14th November 2014.
[2]   Peter Moores Professor of Management Studies, Saïd Business School University of Oxford.
[3]   *Financial Times*, 12 November 2014, www.ft.com/cms/s/0/aa812316-69be-11e4-9f65-00144feabdc0.html?siteedition=uk#slide0.
[4]   See J. ARMOUR, C. MAYER and A. POLO, 2012, *Regulatory Sanctions and Reputational Damage in Financial Markets*, http://papers.ssrn.com/sol3/papers.cfm?abstract_id=1678028.

8.2.   AN EXAMPLE OF A WELL-PERFORMING BANK

One of the most successful banks in Europe is currently Handelsbanken. It needed no bail out in either the financial crisis or the Swedish banking crisis. It is one of the highest equity return banks in Europe. It is one of the fastest expanding banks in the UK[5].

The first feature of the bank is that it pays its employees no bonuses. Recall that we are routinely told that banks have to pay their employees substantial bonuses for them to be able to compete and retain their best people. Well, here is one of the most successful banks earning substantial returns for its shareholders, paying its bankers no bonuses except the share of profits that they receive on retirement from the bank in their pensions.

The second feature of the bank is that it devolves all decision taking down to the level of individual branch managers, including participation of branch managers in decisions about the largest loans. Branches make decisions about all aspects of their activities including which products they sell, how much they charge and how they are advertised. Risk is not in general managed centrally but devolved down to the branches, just as used to be normal practice in banks where branch managers had real authority.

The third feature of Handelsbanken is its shareholding. Its main shareholders are its pension fund, Oktogonen, and Industrivärden, a Swedish investment fund, one of whose largest shareholders is Handelsbanken. So Handelsbanken is part of a cross-shareholding in which control resides within the corporation itself. What would traditionally be deemed to be disastrous corporate governance is associated with highly successful, long-term growth and prosperity of the bank.

8.3.   DO CONVENTIONAL CORPORATE GOVERNANCE
ARRANGEMENTS WORK IN BANKS?

This is not an isolated case. Evidence from the academic literature suggests that those banks with the best corporate governance arrangements according to conventional measures were the ones that failed the most during the financial crisis and those with the highest powered incentives were the ones that took the

---

[5]   See N. KRONER, 2009, *A Blueprint for Better Banking: Svenska Handelsbanken and a Proven Model for More Stable and Profitable Banking*, Petersfield, Harriman House.

greatest risks[6]. Conventional views about corporate governance simply do not apply in relation to either specific examples or evidence from empirical studies of large numbers of banks.

The reason is that in highly leveraged institutions such as banks there is a particularly serious conflict between the two main investors-shareholders and creditors (bondholders and depositors). Shareholders benefit from upside gains but it is the creditors (and ultimately the tax payers in systemically important institutions) who bear the downside losses that force banks into bankruptcy. Remuneration structures that reward management for pursing shareholder interests are in conflict with those of creditors.

8.4. DECENTRALIZATION WORKS BETTER THAN RISK COMMITTEES

Of course it is perfectly possible to control risks through imposition of sufficiently rigorous restrictions. The evidence is that banks with strong risk controls took fewer risks than other banks during the financial crisis[7]. That is not entirely surprising. The Soviet Republic was able to control risks through imprisoning those who took it. The question is, is it desirable to manage risks centrally through risk committees and risk officers.

The answer is sometimes but in general no. The first point is that, while it can be done, it is difficult to do well. Anyone who has been involved in risk committees knows how difficult it is to monitor risks centrally. Just as the Soviet Republic collapsed through the impossibility of the information exercise it was trying to perform, so risk committees are prone to failure because of the complexity of the management task that they are trying to undertake.

Second, central management of risk is a source of systemic risk itself not a way of mitigating it. If risk is managed centrally then when a failure emerges in one part of the bank it will be indicative of an institutional failure throughout because everyone is following the same management practices. It is similar to the argument suggesting that systemic risk is created when central banks and regulators impose prescriptive management rules on banks[8]. As soon as one bank

---

6   A. BELTRATTI and R. STULZ, 2012, "The Credit Crisis Around the Globe: Why Did Some Banks Perform Better?" *Journal of Financial Economics*; D. ERKEN, M. HUNG and P. MATOS, 2012, "Corporate Governance in the 2007-2007 Financial Crisis: Evidence from Financial Institutions Worldwide", *Journal of Corporate Finance*; and B. MINTON, J. TAILLARD and R. WILLIAMSON, 2014, "Financial Expertise of the Board, Risk Taking and Performance: Evidence from Bank Holding Companies", *Journal of Financial and Quantitative Analysis*.
7   A. ELLUL and V. YERRAMILLI, 2013, "Stronger Risk Controls, Lower Risk: Evidence from U.S. Bank Holding Companies", *Journal of Finance*.
8   A. MORRISON and L. WHITE, 2013, "Reputational Contagion and Optimal Regulatory Forbearance", *Journal of Financial Economics*.

fails then the market should quite correctly infer that the whole apple cart is rotten because everyone is managing risks in the same way.

Third, just as the Soviet controlled risk at the expense of innovation so too centralized risk committees discourage banks from doing what they should be doing. They start from the presumption that the purpose of a bank is to limit risk. That is as wrong as the converse argument that the purpose of a bank is to maximize its shareholders value.

The purpose of a bank is to do things. To lend money, to screen and monitor borrowers, in particular where financial markets cannot or do not perform these functions. Criticism of British banking's failure to support small and medium sized companies has become more vocal since the financial crisis of 2008. That is exactly what one would expect. If risk control is regarded a primary objective and banks are penalized for taking it by being required to hold capital in proportion to their risk-weighted assets then they stop taking risks.

So the starting point behind risk committees is wrong. But so too is its approach. The way that Handelsbanken became a highly prudent, safe bank was not through its risk committee. It was exactly the opposite. It was through delegating not centralizing decision taking. How did it do that? Two things. First it devoted a great deal of effort and attention to selecting people – people it could trust to act intelligently, prudently and according to the principles and values of the bank. Second, it instilled a strong common culture about the purpose and values of the bank so that everyone was aware of how they were supposed to behave and what was acceptable conduct.

That is the way in which every successful organization in the world works. It is the way in which we bring up our families and children. We don't employ a risk committee to manage them. We educate and instil a strong sense of purpose and then we leave them to get on and run their own lives. Successful organizations operate in exactly the same way.

There are two exceptions. The first is when those in whom we have placed trust fail us. That is what has happened during the financial crisis. The result was the largest banks in Britain were effectively if not formally placed in administration. And because banks no longer trusted those working for them, they effectively in turn put their entire organizations into 'special measures' transferring oversight and control to central committees and boards. As a short-term expedient it may have been necessary but as a way of running a bank it is disastrous. It extinguishes innovation, it creates systemic risk within banks and across financial institutions and it stops banks doing what they are supposed to be doing.

If risk committees and risk officers were the ways of avoiding bank failures, it is hard to imagine that they would not have been invented some 700 years ago when banks first became established in Europe. That is not to say they should never be observed anymore than it is correct to say that central banks should never be involved in overseeing bank risks. They have a vital role to play in relation to one specific type of risk-aggregate systemic risk. Those risks that individual banks or individual divisions or branches of banks cannot observe or control themselves need to be centrally monitored and managed. A failure to do so is a failure to internalize an important externality within and across institutions and an abrogation of responsibility on the part of both banks and central banks.

That is what the board and risk committees of well-run banks like Handelsbanken do. They are embedded in the banks' strategy to avoid excessive concentrations of activity in particular areas, to provide early warning of where risk concentrations are becoming excessive, to insure that those aggregate risks are hedged through insurance, to be able to establish whether failures are due to idiosyncratic random losses or a failure of management, and where it is the latter to intervene and change management. That is precisely what central risk committees should be doing within organizations and what the central bank should be doing in relation to the financial system as a whole.

But that is a very different mind-set from saying that the purpose of a risk committee is to control risk. The only thing that we know from evidence on corporate governance and boards is that we do not know. We do not know what is the right way of managing risks. And the reason we do not know is that there is not a right way or a single best form of corporate governance and we should stop behaving as if there was. We should start to learn from cases of success such as Handelsbanken that there is not a simple toolkit for managing bank risks.

9. CORPORATE GOVERNANCE OF BANKS ACCORDING TO THE CRD IV

Eddy Wymeersch[1]

It has often been stated – and sometimes overstated – that poor corporate governance in banks has been one of the factors leading to the financial crisis. It is undeniable that certain aspects of weak governance have contributed to the crisis, but to assume causation would certainly be overdone. Banks, as was alleged, were poorly managed, with insufficiently expert boards with insufficient knowledge of the bank's activity, its structure or its risk profile, too risk minded – for some with a reference to excessive bonuses or to unbalanced gender diversity – too focused on short term profits, driven by a remuneration system that induced over-risky behaviour, and so on[2]. As was discovered after the crisis, compliance with laws and regulations was substandard, sometimes amounting to clearly criminal behaviour, while practices were revealed that constituted abuse in clear violation of the long-term interests of the financial system, of the national economy that it was supposed to serve and ultimately to the detriment of market participants. Heavy fines have been inflicted, while a significant number of individuals have whether been sentenced or definitively removed from the financial world. In certain cases, as have been widely discussed in the press, the names of some banks could be placed next to each of these points. But that does not mean that all banks have misbehaved.

Corporate governance rules can contribute to give an answer to these concerns. However at the end of the day, it is personal integrity, a clear view on societal responsibilities and a higher view on the overall function of the financial system that should contribute to a healthier but also stronger financial system. Morals will not suffice so that in the meantime, we have to live with additional laws, regulations, codes of conduct and stricter enforcement in the hope that these will result in improving people's conduct[3]. This is exactly what has happened in both the US (see the Dodd Frank Act) as in the European Union (CRD IV), where stricter legislation has been adopted. The relationship between bank governance and financial risk has been extensively studied and analysed. The purpose of this

---

[1] University of Gent – ECGI Fellow.
[2] See on the causes of excessive risk taking: M. BECHT, P. BOLTON and A. ROELL, "Bank governance is different", *Oxford review of economic policy*, 27, 2011, 444, mentioning that shareholders did not oppose (at 452); R. FAHLENBRACH and R. STULZ, "Bank CEO incentives and the credit crisis", *J. Financial Economics*, 98 (2011) 11-26 refuted the interest alignment theory: the more stock a bank CEO held, the worse the performance; greater alignment caused worse performance (at 453).
[3] See the proposals published in the UK: BoE and FCA Strengthening accountability in banking: a new regulatory framework for individuals, FCA CP14/13/PRA CP14/14, Sir Richard Lambert launches UK banking standards council, FT, 19 May 2014.

paper is to give a more technical overview of this legislation with some critical footnotes attached. Therefore no description or analysis will be made of all the evils that beset the financial world in the past[4].

Formulating the optimal format for bank governance after the crisis has been repeatedly dealt with by the international financial authorities, such as the Financial Stability Board and the Basel Committee[5], who rightly extended the link between governance mechanisms and 'risk' in all its aspects. Many of these ideas have been translated in the European Commission's early work on the subject, as formulated in its recommendations[6]. Addressed to the EU Member States, the effectiveness of these recommendations has been limited as the states generally have been weak in transposition into internal law. As could be expected, the next step consisted of upgrading the provisions into binding legal instruments: this has been done mainly in the Capital Requirements Directives III and IV (CRD III and IV) and to a lesser extent in some other instruments[7].

By 'upgrading' the governance regime, the EU legislator has considerably modified the applicable governance system: where before the CRD IV, governance was a matter dealt with essentially in company law, and further implemented in the company's internal rules, in its articles of incorporation, with some additional internal codes of conduct, in its by-laws, (often based on the corporate governance codes for listed companies), the new regime confers to several of these rules the status of supervisory rules, superseding any contrary internal provisions, and imposed, monitored or approved by the prudential supervisor. From private law, the regime has changed into public, supervisory law. Breaches of the rules will expose companies and individuals to supervisory sanctions, such as being declared 'unfit or improper' and as a consequence sometimes being expelled from the financial sector. If provided in national law, fines can be imposed. Civil

---

[4]   For a broad overview see G. FERRARINI and M.C. UNGUREANU, "Executive Remuneration. A Comparative Overview", *ECGI Law Working Paper* No. 268/2014; G. FERRARINI, *CRD IV and the mandatory structure of bankers' pay: Rules v. Standards* (2014 to be published).

[5]   BCBS Enhancing corporate governance for banking organisations, September 1999, superseded by Corporate governance principles for banks, Guidelines, Consultative document, October 2014. On risk management: FSB, Thematic Review on Risk Governance, Peer review report, 12 February 2013; FSB Principles for An Effective Risk Appetite Framework, 18 November 2013; Senior Supervisors Group (ssg), Observations on Developments in Risk Appetite Frameworks and IT Infrastructure, December, 23 2010; SSG, 2009: Observations on the risk management practices, www.newyorkfed.org/newsevents/news/banking/2008/SSG Risk Mgt doc final.pdf.

[6]   See Commission Recommendation 2009/384/EC of 30 April 2009 on remuneration policies in the financial services sector (*OJ*.L. 120, 15 May 2009, p. 22), Commission recommendation of 9 April 2014 on the quality of corporate governance reporting ('comply or explain') *OJ*.L. 109/43, 12 April 2014; for the older recommendations: see Commission recommendations 2004/913 fostering an appropriate regime for the remuneration of directors of listed companies, *OJ*.L. 385/55, 29 December 2004 and 2005/162/EC the role of non-executive or supervisory directors of listed companies and on the committees of the (supervisory) board, *OJ*.L. 52/51, 25 February 2005; Commission Communication accompanying Commission Recommendation 2009/384 of 30 April 2009 complementing Recommendations 2004/913/EC and 2005/162/EC as regards the regime for the remuneration of directors of listed companies and Commission Recommendation on remuneration policies in the financial services sector, http://ec.europa.eu/internal_market/company/docs/directors-remun/COM%282009%29_211_EN.pdf.

[7]   See e.g. in the takeover directive 2004/25 of 21 April 2004 on takeover bids, *OJ*.L. 142/12, 30 April 2004, or in the directive on financial conglomerates on related party transactions (nt 3).

liability for breaches of the rules will occur, and this according to the general national liability rules. Corporate governance will have moved from a flexible, self-defined rather accommodating set of concepts, largely of an ethical nature, to hard and fast supervisory rules, enforced by prudential supervisors if needed by imposing severe sanctions. The climate has changed: massive fines were imposed, rarely for breaching the governance rules, but for a lack of integrity, unethical conduct if not for outright violations of the law.

This considerable strengthening of the banks' governance regime is largely due to the financial crisis[8]. Strikingly, the base line for formalising the governance provisions is the overarching concern with risk taking. In each of the CRD IV's governance provision, reference is made to risk. The traditional concept that governance deals with the relation of shareholders with the company, with the position and functioning of board of directors in relationship with the management, and this in an overall perspective of creating shareholder value, is largely unmentioned. There is barely any mention of shareholders.

Risk considerations dominate the regulatory approach: governance is used as a factor allowing risk to be reduced, mitigated, covered, and in general kept under control ("risk appetite"). This approach is especially significant in its relation to the remuneration of management: the new, strict rules are intended to avoid excessive risks to be undertaken, not to reduce the remuneration paid.

9.1. THE EUROPEAN REGULATORY FRAMEWORK

Corporate governance has been the subject of repeated statements by the European bodies: originally these mostly took the form of recommendations, addressed to the Member States. The follow-up was rather mixed, although the concepts laid down in these recommendations where sometimes included in the national legislations. The extent to which these recommendations have some legally relevant force would deserve further analysis[9]. At the same time, recommendations continue to play an important role, although their source may be one of the ESAs or European Supervisory Authorities[10].

More specifically, with respect to the corporate governance of banks, the main sources of legislation are the Capital Requirement Directives III and IV and the Capital Requirements Regulation[11]. But other sources should also be taken into

---

[8]   M. BECHT, P. BOLTON and A. ROELL, *Bank governance is different*, nt. 1.
[9]   See ECJ 19 December 1989, C-322/88 on the binding nature of Commission recommendations.
[10] See Commission recommendation 15 February 2005, *OJ.L.* 52/51, 25 February 2005.
[11] Directive 2013/36 of 26 June 2013 on access to the activity of credit institutions and the prudential supervision of credit institutions and investment firms, *OJ.L.* 176/338, 27 June 2013, (CRD IV). Regulation 575/2013 on prudential requirement for credit institutions and investment firms, 26 June 2013, *OJ.L.* 176/1, 27 June 2013, (CRR).

account: the insurance legislation, especially Solvency II[12], and the Financial Conglomerates Directives[13] contain significant provisions dealing with governance in their respective fields. With respect to the securities world, apart from the provisions of the Shareholder Rights directive[14], and of the Transparency directive, special mention deserves the provisions of the Investment Funds directives[15], and of the Alternative Investment Fund Management directive[16], which provisions have built on concepts developed in the banking directives. These different instruments are likely to play a role in determining the rules applicable to banks, especially in the context of larger financial services groups, where some form of 'regulatory contagion' or 'arbitration' may take place. In addition, general company law measures remain generally applicable.

It would be misleading to consider that the governance of banks is entirely contained in the provisions of the European legislation. There is a considerable body of law, regulation, techniques and analysis that is situated at the national level[17].

9.2.   THE NEW REGULATORY CONTEXT

Before these regulatory interventions, banks decided about their corporate governance structure within the context of the applicable company law, supplemented by internal conduct rules. For listed banks, the corporate governance

---

[12]   Directive 2009/138 of 25 November 2009, *OJ.L.EU* 335/1, 17 December 2009, Solvency II. Directive 2012/23 of 12 September 2012, *OJ.L.EU* 249/1, 14 September 2012 (postponing Solvency II). Commission delegated regulation. ...Amending Directive 2008/138 of 10 October 2014, C (2014) 7230 Final, 10 October 2014) on remuneration.

[13]   Directive 2002/87 of 16 December 2002 on the supplementary supervision of credit institutions, insurance undertakings and investment firms in a financial conglomerate, *OJ.L.EU* 35/1, 11 February 2002, modified by Directive 2010/78/EU of 24 November 2010 (Omnibus 1); Directive 2011/89 of 16 November 2011 as regards supplementary supervision of financial entities in a financial conglomerate, *OJ.L.EU* 326/113, 8 December 2011.

[14]   See directive 2004/109/EC of 15 December 2004 on the harmonisation of transparency requirements in relation to information about issuers whose securities are admitted to trading on a regulated market and amending Directive 2001/34/EU, *OJ.L.* 390/38, 31 December 2004; Directive 2013/50 of 22 October 2013, amending directive 2004/109.... *OJ.L.EU* 294/13, 6 November 2013, and the changes proposed in: European Commission, amending Directive 2007/36/EC as regards the encouragement of long-term shareholder engagement and Directive 2013/34/EU as regards certain elements of the corporate governance statement (2014/0121COD).

[15]   UCITS IV and V: Directive 2009/65/EC of the European Parliament and of the Council of 13 July 2009 on the coordination of laws, regulations and administrative provisions relating to undertakings for collective investment in transferable securities (UCITS) (*OJ.L* 302, 17 November 2009, p. 32). Directive 2014/91/EU of 23 July 2014 amending Directive 2009/65/EC on the coordination of laws, regulations and administrative provisions relating to undertakings for collective investment in transferable securities (UCITS) as regards depositary functions, remuneration policies and sanctions (Ucits V), *OJ.L.* 257/196, 28 Augustus 2014.

[16]   Directive 2011/61/EU of the European Parliament and of the Council of 8 June 2011 on Alternative Investment Fund Managers and amending Directives 2003/41/EC and 2009/65/EC and Regulations (EC) No. 1060/2009 and (EU) No. 1095/2010 (*OJ.L.* 174, 1 July 2011, p. 1) (AIFMD).

[17]   See for a thorough analysis, mainly under German law, K.J. HOPT and G. WOHLMANNSTETTER (eds), *Handbuch Corporate Governance*, 2011, 776 p., Vahlen and Beck Verlaege. For the European legal analysis, see K.J. HOPT, "Corporate governance of banks and other financial institutions after the financial crisis", *Journal of Corporate Law Studies*, October 2013, 219.

codes were taken into account, although on a 'comply or explain' basis. In some cases, individual external review of governance practices was undertaken by the prudential supervisor. Mention should be made of the review exercises undertaken with respect to the full range of listed companies – including banking groups – on the basis of their 'comply or explain' publications[18].

Much of this has been changed after the adoption of the CRD III and IV[19], or more specifically after their implementation in national legislation. The resulting governance regime is now mandatory and is subject to assessment within the general supervisory review process. Financial supervisors are actively involved in checking governance provisions within banks, especially on the basis of the banks' governance statements. The corporate governance rules as developed in the corporate governance codes have lost much – but by no means all – of their significance. They continue to be useful in guiding boards for matters that are not, or very generally addressed in the legislation. A good example is the subject of conflicts of interest[20], a matter that is only referred to in the CRD IV but usually governed by detailed provisions whether in national company law or in governance codes. On many other points a reference to a governance code is considered good practice and certainly gives support to board decisions.

The statement that the governance rules have become 'mandatory' has to be qualified. Usually their direct source will be the national law. At the level of the European directive, the core obligations of a banking group are stated not in formal or legally binding rules – a certain number important exceptions notwithstanding – but by way of 'governance arrangements' that relate to the essential duties of a board[21]. These arrangements will refer to the board's overall responsibility for dealing with "strategic objectives, risk strategy and internal governance", while ensuring the integrity of the accounting, reporting, internal controls and compliance processes. Effective oversight of the management and oversight of disclosure and communications belong to the same core duties. By referring to 'arrangements' to be developed by the banks themselves, the directive leaves ample freedom for national legislators whether to prescribe the format the board will have to adopt or to let the banks adopt governance mechanisms that are fully adapted to their individual or specific needs, always under supervisory oversight. The position of the executive committee can vary: it is a separate body

---

18 See about the monitoring of corporate governance codes: WYMEERSCH, "European Corporate Governance Codes and their effectiveness" in BELCREDI and FERRARINI (eds.) *Boards and Shareholders in European Listed Companies, Facts, Context and Post-Crisis Reforms*, Cambridge University Press, 2013.

19 Directive 2010/76/EU of the European Parliament and of the Council of 24 November 2010 amending Directives 2006/48/EC and 2006/49/EC as regards capital requirements for the trading book and for re-securitisations, and the supervisory review of remuneration policies, OJ.L.EU 329/3, 14 December 2010.

20 See art. 88, § 1 CRD IV; compare the provisions in the Financial Conglomerates directives, nt. 3, on intra-group transactions (art. 8).

21 Art. 88, CRD IV.

in the two-tier boards systems, while in others the committee, or the executives must – or may – be part of the board.

In the approach of the directive, these governance arrangements are to be further developed by the 'management body'. The task of the supervisors is to ensure that the "management body monitors and regularly assesses the effectiveness of the governance arrangements…"[22].

9.3. STRUCTURING THE BOARD

The Directive contains some provisions on the way a bank board should be structured. The provisions – as implemented by the national legislator – apply to 'an institution' i.e. to each individual bank. In a group context, this provision is likely to create difficulties as it seem excessive to require the same provisions to be applied at the level of each of the subsidiaries, there where in practice most of these are managed on an integrated basis. If for instance, different rules apply to risk monitoring or to compliance, group-wide compliance may have difficulties in imposing a group view. While the directive contains provisions on consolidated supervision, or on the inclusion of mixed financial holding companies in consolidated supervision, it does not extend the governance provisions to all group companies[23]. This will make group integrated management more difficult, what may be a risk factor.

A certain flexibility is needed not only from a governance point of view but also to take account of the very different governance structures in national company law. This idea is reflected in the directive's choice for the term 'management body', expressly defined in a neutral way as to include one or two-tier boards or any other formula, and including the executive directors. National traditions of board composition are widely different, some including the executives, others limiting it to the CEO, while some even excluding any executive presence, except in an advisory role.

As the general definition of 'management body' did not allow for sufficient identification of the supervisory role of the board, both executives and non-executives often being members in the same board, the directive adds a term referring to the "management body in its supervisory function" meaning "the management body acting in its role of overseeing and monitoring management decision making"[24].

---

[22]   Art. 88, § 1, 2nd section, CRD IV.
[23]   See art. 111 e.s. and especially 120, CRD IV, referring to the directives on financial conglomerates. The 'fit and proper' test shall also apply to the directors of the mixed financial holding company.
[24]   Art. 3 (1) (7) and (8), CRD IV.

As a consequence, the directive distinguishes only between executives and non-executives, the latter ones being called upon to compose the specialised committees. The independent directors are not mentioned as a separate class and will be considered 'non-executives'. This provision would not prevent national legislators to require a minimum presence of independent members.

The procedure for appointing these classes of directors is mentioned in the directive by reference to the institution, within the board, of a nomination committee, with wider competences than proposing candidates for appointment. Companies where the management body plays no role in appointment – closely held companies most of the time – can disregard the obligation to appoint a nomination committee. In both cases however the role of the general meeting is left untouched; here company law will apply.

The regulatory conditions for appointing directors are the usual ones: the traditional fit and proper test will apply, supplemented by conditions relating to the members' "sufficient knowledge, skills and experience", conditions to be verified by the supervisor. To be mentioned is the reference to the gender policy to be applied within the management body[25] but without differentiation between executives and non-executives.

The 'four eyes principle' is expressly mentioned with respect to executives, but without specifying how far it extends and which decisions are subject to the requirement[26]. Here internal decision could play a supplementary role.

The position of the chairman of the board is not controversial in most EU jurisdictions: he is a non-executive. But in some states – France being a prominent example –, the CEO can also chair the board: this practice has been declared permissible in the directive but only if it is justified by the bank and is authorised by the supervisor[27].

A somewhat puzzling statement is the one whereby the nomination committee should "take account of the need to ensure that.... decision making is not dominated by any one individual or small group of individuals in a manner that is detrimental to the interest of the institution as a whole"[28]. One can read this statement in the context of the observation, in the preamble to this Directive, about 'group think'[29] although a requirement for a balanced board would probably have been more adequate.

---

[25] Art. 88 (2) (a) CRD IV, referring to a decision of the nomination committee – probably to be confirmed by the management body – and calling for a target for representation of the underrepresented gender. This measure will be supplemented by the provisions of the forthcoming directives on gender representation.

[26] Art. 13(1), CRD IV.

[27] Art. 88 (1) (e), CRD IV.

[28] Art. 88 (2) 2nd §, CRD IV. This provision might apply to the predominant representation of a controlling shareholder.

[29] See Preamble § 60, CRD IV.

9.4.   BOARD COMMITTEES

The European directives mandate the constitution, within the board, of four internal committees. This regime applies to banks that are "significant in terms of size, internal organisation and nature scope and complexity of activities". This definition of a 'significant' institution is comparable to the one followed in the SSM Regulation but significant institutions under the SSM will also qualify under the CRD IV definition. The directive requires these committees to be organised in each of the group entities, and does not provide for group committees. In practice however, audit and risk should also be monitored on a group-wide basis. Coordination between the group committees and the single entity committees should be provided and will support consolidated supervision.

Audit Committees are mandatory for Public Interest Entities on the basis of the Accounting directive[30]: they should be composed of non-executive directors. The chairman shall be independent and one other independent director should have competences in accounting and/or auditing[31].

The Risk Committee is composed of non-executive directors, which have sufficient knowledge to judge the risk strategy and the risk appetite of the bank. The Committee will advise the management, but the latter will remain responsible for the overall risk profile. This is especially important as the Committee will review the pricing of the bank products or services, taking into account its business model and risk strategy. In smaller institutions, the risk and audit committee functions may be merged into one committee, normally the audit committee.

Banks have to organise a risk management function, independent from the management[32]. This requirement essentially refers to the risk function, but could also be applied to other control functions such as compliance, or internal audit. Independence from management and direct access to relevant information are declared applicable to the management function[33]. Direct reporting or access to the board in its supervisory mode should be provided[34]. Proportionality is explicitly mentioned by reference to the specific provisions of directive 2006/73[35] relating to investment firms.

---

[30]   Art. 41, Directive 2006/43 as modified by art. 39, Directive 2014/56.
[31]   All members have to be independent of that audited entity, but are not necessarily independent directors for that.
[32]   Art. 76 (5), CRV IV. Compare art. 92(2)(d) applicable to all control staff and their variable remuneration.
[33]   Art. 76 (4) CRD IV.
[34]   See art. 76 (5).
[35]   Commission directive 2006/73/EC of 10 August 2006 implementing Directive 2004/39/EC of the European Parliament and of the Council as regards organisational requirements and operating conditions for investment firms and defined terms for the purposes of that Directive 2 September 2006, L. 241/26, with i.a. detailed provisions on internal audit and risk management.

Interesting is the position of the risk manager: although not expressly mentioned, he should take part in the meetings of the risk committee, and in any case has always direct access to the board, where he can 'raise concerns or warn'. The directive qualifies him as an independent senior manager with separate responsibility for risk management and who can act with sufficient 'authority, stature'. He should have 'adequate resources' under his command. Although he is fully part of the management, he is protected against dismissal by the management: a dismissal should be subject to the prior approval of the board, acting in supervisory mode, i.e. without the executives being present. The remuneration of the senior officers in the risk and compliance lines is directly overseen by the remuneration committee, and not by the general management[36]. Their remuneration is the subject of a special protective regime: although their remuneration can be linked to the achievements of the objectives linked to their function, it should remain unrelated to the business activity under their control. This rule applies to all staff in control functions, such as compliance or internal audit as these should be independent from the activity they oversee as well. Often these rules will be developed in more detail in the internal governance memorandum. The prudential supervisor will closely follow whether these provisions are effectively applied, but also more generally whether the control functions have adequate powers to intervene in the management and where needed, can timely oppose certain transactions or developments.

The Nomination Committee is also composed of non-executives, and proposes nominations to the board. It is in charge of following up on the board activities, assess the individual members and review the policies for selection and appointment of senior managers. Its involvement in gender diversity has been mentioned above.

The Remuneration committee plays an important role in the increasingly complex matter of preparing remuneration decisions. Its composition has been framed more widely: executives and non-executives may be part provided the committee, as a whole will be able to exercise competent and independent judgment on remuneration[37]. Remuneration decisions, both in terms of policies and individual decisions are prepared by this committee, but the final decision remains the competence of the board.

The directive states that the decisions of this Committee should reflect "the long-term interest of shareholders, investors and other stakeholders in the

---

[36]   Or where no such committee has been established, by the board in supervisory mode. Art. 95(2) defines the role of the remuneration committee and of the board in fixing their remuneration.

[37]   Already mentioned in Directive 2010/76/EU of the European Parliament and of the Council of 24 November 2010 amending Directives 2006/48/EC and 2006/49/EC as regards capital requirements for the trading book and for re-securitisations, and the supervisory review of remuneration policies, annex I.

institution"[38], and also the 'public interest'. How this provision has to be understood will be the subject of controversy: the broad formulation probably refers to the awareness of the relation between remuneration and the bank's risk profile, as excessive risk taking may affect the different interests mentioned, while the reference to the 'public interest' can be read as a reference to the financial stability concerns of remuneration-driven excessive risk-taking. Apart from the question whether, apart from instructions from the competent oversight bodies in charge of financial stability, boards should adapt their decisions to possible financial stability concerns – on which they will usually not be very well informed – will be difficult. Legally at least, these public interest considerations will only intervene at the level of the advice of the remuneration committee and not be binding on the board which will have the last word in this matter. With respect to the board decision itself, there is no regulatory requirement to adapt its decisions – on remuneration or on any other subject – to issues involving financial stability. Informal supervisory action may come into play here.

These different committees will only act in an advisory mode recommending necessary action to the board. However, the directive contains at least one reference to a decision-making competence i.e. where the board cannot overrule the committee decision. This would be the case for the Nomination Committee on gender policy, where the committee will 'decide on a target' and a policy for balanced gender representation[39].

9.5.   INTERNAL GOVERNANCE

The directive deals with ' internal governance' processes with respect to mechanisms on the one hand for dealing with risks, on the other with recovery and resolution. The latter fields have later been expanded in the directive on recovery and resolution or BRRD, and will not be commented on here[40].

There are a certain number of internal governance processes and instruments that are mentioned under this heading, that relate to "robust governance arrangement" or a "clear organisational structure with the internal mechanism instituted to ensure "well defined, transparent and consistent lines of responsibility"[41], These processes are essentially focused on identifying and monitoring the bank's risks: it is up to the management body to define the risk profile, and to approve and review

---

[38]   This terminology was used in the BCBS, Principles for enhancing corporate governance, October 2010.
[39]   Art. 88 (2) (a), CRD IV.
[40]   Directive 2014/59/EU of 15 May 2014 establishing a framework for the recovery and resolution of credit institutions and investment firms and amending Council Directive 82/891/EEC, and Directives 2001/24/EC, 2002/47/EC, 2004/25/EC, 2005/56/EC, 2007/36/EC, 2011/35/EU, 2012/30/EU and 2013/36/EU, and Regulations (EU) No. 1093/2010 and (EU) No. 648/2012, of the European Parliament and of the Council, OJ.L. 173/190, 12 June 2014 (BRRD).
[41]   Art. 74, CRD IV.

the strategies and policies relating to risks including their occurrence within the macroeconomic environment. In smaller institutions, risk surveillance should be undertaken in the board itself, unless a risk committee is instituted in combination with the audit committee[42]. In larger, significant institutions a risk committee will have to be organised.

The duties of the boards and other parties involved in the internal management of a banking group have been described in the Basel Committee paper on 'Enhancing Corporate Governance'. With regard to group structures, the BCBS formulates as Principle No. 4:

> *"In a group structure, the board of the parent company has the overall responsibility for adequate corporate governance across the group and ensuring that there are governance policies and mechanisms appropriate to the structure, business and risks of the group and its entities".*

The directive contains a comparable obligation as to the duties and responsibilities of the Board, but does not clarify whether these requirements would also be applicable on a group basis[43]. Although in practice they will often be applied on a consolidated basis, there are some concerns that a group integrated approach might be incompatible with company law, where in several EU jurisdictions a clear separation of legal entities being part of the group is the prevailing legal opinion. Interference with another group company's management may be a source of risk, going up to parent company liability. This issue has also been mentioned in the proposals to reform the Financial Conglomerates directive and considered a handicap for further integrating supervision on a full conglomerate basis[44].

9.6. THE DIRECTIVE PROVISIONS LIMITING ADDITIONAL DIRECTORSHIPS AND REMUNERATION

The CRD IV contains two series of provisions that contain strict obligations affecting the position of board members: the first one relates to the limitation of additional mandates for board members (9.7.), the second relates to the remuneration of board members and other identified staff (9.8.).

The terminology in which these provisions have been cast call for a preliminary question: both provisions have been stated as directly addressing board members, or in the case of the remuneration provision as a limiting the powers of the banks

---

[42]   The latter is imposed by art. 41 of directive 2006/43, now repealed.
[43]   Art. 88 (1)(a).
[44]   Commission Staff Working Documents, Report on the review of the directive 2002/87, 15 March 2013, SWD (2013) 71 Final, p. 11.

to set a certain ratio exceeding the directive's remuneration ceiling. This formulation seems different from that normally used in directives which are addressed to Member States. Should one therefore consider that these provisions have the status of a regulation, directly applicable in the national legal order, but also binding on the Member States?

9.7.   LIMITATIONS ON THE NUMBER OF DIRECTORSHIPS

The directive contains a series of detailed provisions based on the idea that directors in the past did not commit themselves sufficiently to the bank's business: "all members of the management body should commit sufficient time to perform their functions in the board" states article 91(2). This statement has not been based on hard evidence. There were some cases where bank directors did not have sufficient knowledge of the bank's structure, or of its different business activities. Many bank publish tables of board attendance, and these have shown cases of repeated absence but this should have been solved by inviting repeated sinners by its natural sanction, i.e. to attend or leave the board more or less voluntarily. The directive formulated the requirement in terms of time commitment, an essentially quantitative criterion. Whether more time commitment guarantees a better qualitative input from the directors present cannot be affirmed in general terms. It would have been preferable that the principle having been stated, the supervisory review process would have traced the limits for board attendance and commitment.

This principle has been expanded by a European Parliament initiative in the final version of the directive by adopting a quantitative limit on the number of directorships a bank director can hold[45]. It should be remarked from the outset that the rule applies per individual bank, with however important group exceptions. Also the provision does not seem to exclude national legislation to provide for stricter conditions.

With respect to executive directors, the directive provides that an executive director may not hold more than two additional non-executive directorships. The non-executive directors are limited to three other directorships, and these may only be non-executive as well.

The directive contains some exceptions, mainly for directorships held as representative of a Member State[46], or in not-for-profit organisations, the main exception relating to directorships held within the group. It is indeed logical for

---

[45]   The French companies legislation contains a comparable requirement, but than applicable to all companies: "une personne physique ne peut exercer simultanément plus de cinq mandats d'administrateur de sociétés anonymes ayant leur siège sur le territoire français", art. L 225-21 of the Code de commerce.
[46]   Excluding from this exemption are directors that represent state owned entities, such as sovereign wealth funds.

the group top management to be member of the different entities of which the group is composed and this in order to monitor and coordinate group action.

The way the directive provisions have been formulated leads to a couple of question marks. The first is one of internal logic and relates to the comparable treatment of executives and non-executives: there where executives have the right to exercise two additional functions, leading to a quite heavy workload in addition to their main executive activities, non-executives are limited to four in total, although they should in principle be more available than executives. If, by way of hypothesis, an executive position could be considered to stand for a 90% time commitment, and a non-executive one for 25%, this would mean that executives could be active for more than 140%, while non-executives are limited to 100%. The explanation for this approach is not clear.

The restrictions introduced by the directive do not seem to provide that these apply first in the bank, and create limitations for directorships in other companies. They could also be read in the reverse order. This would lead to the illogical outcome that a CEO of a non-banking company, who sits on the board of a bank in a non-executive capacity, can only hold three other non-executive positions outside the bank, in fact leading to his resignation as a CEO, or more likely as a bank director. This reading would result in eliminating able and experienced businessmen from taking part in the direction of banks. This solution is illogical and should be remedied.

A similar reasoning may apply to a director of a group insurance company: the Solvency II insurance directive does not contain similar restrictions on the number of mandates that their directors can hold. However, insurance executives will be severely restricted if they hold a directorship in the banking entity, e.g. the parent bank, as in that case that position will result in incompatibility with an executive position on the insurance side. This feature may contribute to splitting up the management of bank-insurance groups, what may be contrary to the business scheme underlying the group.

Among the exceptions to the rule, those relating to directorships in group entities deserve special attention: it states that directorships in group companies will "count as a single directorship". The exemption allows bank executives to sit on all subsidiaries' boards, without differentiating between executive and non-executives position. It also allows non-executives to be part of several subsidiary boards, and as no additional conditions have been posed, they could act as executives in the group entities as well. Many will consider this as an anomaly, as group non-executives should not be involved in managing subsidiaries out of fear of self-review. As non-executives of the parent, their role is also to check the way the management operates, e.g. in terms of risk policy.

The absence of a group definition may also lead to discussions in the actual application of the rule. Usually the group notion will be defined be reference to the accounting directives, in this case the directive on consolidated accounts[47]. This directive uses for defining dependent group entities the power of the parent to determine the decisions to be taken by the subsidiary, whether on the basis of majority control of the voting shares, or by contractual techniques allowing the parent to cast the majority of the votes. If in the absence of the voting majority, the parent has the right to appoint of dismiss the members of the subsidiary board, control will be subsumed. Therefore, apart from legal control, also 'de facto' control will allow the subsidiary to be counted to the group. There is a presumption that a 20% holding would suffice to establish control, in the absence of any other, more important shareholder[48]. Although not related to the group definition, the directive further exempts directorships in entities in which the parent holds a 'qualifying holding', i.e. a holding at a lower percentage, even as low as 10%[49]. The combination of these two different levels of control will lead to exempt most related entities from the restrictions on multiple directorships. There is no limitation on the number of group directorships, although the general requirement of 'sufficient time commitment' may restrict even in a group context, too many directorship, to be concentrated in the hands of the same persons.

The directive is unclear whether the restrictions it introduces are a maximum, to be respected by the prudential authorities, or may be further restricted in national legislation. The formulation of the directive, according to which members of the board "shall not hold more than one of the following combinations of directorships at the same time...." seems to indicate that the directive fixed a maximum but that national legislation may provide stricter conditions.

9.8.   REMUNERATION

The most controversial part of the directive relates to the provisions on remuneration. The CRD IV contains detailed provisions on remuneration of bank directors and risk takers, many of them having been carried over from the CRD III[50]. These have largely been inspired by the FSB's Principles for Sound

---

[47]   See art. 1, Seventh Council Directive 83/349/EEC of 13 June 1983 based on the art. 54 (3) (g) of the Treaty on consolidated accounts. The directive does not provide for a delegated act defining the group definition.

[48]   See art. 1 (4), Seventh Council Directive 83/349/EEC of 13 June 1983 based on the art. 54 (3) (g) of the Treaty on consolidated accounts.

[49]   See the definition of "qualified holding" in art. 4(1)(36) of Regulation 575/2013 (CRR).

[50]   Directive 2010/76/EU of the European Parliament and of the Council of 24 November 2010 amending Directives 2006/48/EC and 2006/49/EC as regards capital requirements for the trading book and for re-securitisations, and the supervisory review of remuneration policies CRD III, modifying annex V of the Directive 2006/48.

remuneration practices[51], and its Implementation Standards and the Commission Recommendation of 2009[52]. Some of the material published by the FSB can therefore help to illustrate the European provisions, although the latter are in several respects much stricter and much more detailed.

The objective of the directive's rules on remuneration essentially consists of weakening the link between remuneration and (excessive) risk taking. There is interesting empirical evidence that variable remuneration may have played an important role in additional risk taking, mainly at the level of traders and other risk takers[53]. But one can ask oneself whether the most effective approach to better control excessive risk taking is by regulating remuneration, more specifically by addressing only the variable part of remuneration. Remuneration is best addressed by using governance mechanisms, where 'say on pay' – especially if it has binding force – is a stronger instrument, not dealing with risk taking but directly addressing the amount of the full remuneration[54]. This places the debate at the level where it belongs, i.e. that remuneration should be adapted to the quality of the management or the business activity by the top performers. Activist investors have also proved to be quite effective in exercising pressure for more moderate, overall remuneration. It would therefore be better policy to support remuneration issues with instruments that specifically focus on remuneration, and not confusing it with risk objectives[55]. This does of course not mean that risk has to be neglected but that it should be addressed by the appropriate instruments for controlling risk, several of which are now being developed.

The provisions on remuneration are on the one hand cast in terms of remuneration policies while on the other contain very specific and binding restrictions, especially with respect to the ratio between fixed and variable remuneration. While the policies have to be developed by each bank – more specially on the advice of its remuneration committee[56] – compliance with the directive's provision and further implementing regulations will be supervised by the competent supervisor, in this case the supervisor in charge of the supervision of the group.

---

[51] FSF Principles for Sound Compensation Practices, 2 April 2009, *www.financialstabilityboard.org/publications/r_0904b.pdf*, and the Implementation Standards, 25 September 2009.

[52] Commission Recommendation of 30 April 2009 on remuneration policies in the financial services sector, OJ.L.EU 120/22, 15 May 2009.

[53] See EFING, HAU, KAMPKOETER and STEINBRECHER, *Incentive Pay and Bank-Risk-taking, Evidence from Austrian German and Swiss Banks* 2014, www.nber.org/papers/w20468; http://ssrn.com/abstract=2526325.

[54] See among many C. BRYANT and A. MASSOUDI, "Hard landing looms for golden parachute deals", *FT* 15 January 2015.

[55] On Say on Pay, see "The Proposal for a Directive of the European Parliament and of the Council on improving the gender balance among directors of companies listed on stock exchanges and related measures", 2014/0121 (COD).

[56] See art. 95, CRDIV.

The second and most sensitive series of provisions consist of direct and specific injunctions to national legislators and supervisors to introduce strict restrictions on variable remuneration, as provided for in the directive, or more severe ones if these have been laid down in their national legal system. There is no overall cap on remuneration, as was proposed in some states[57].

In both layers of remuneration, the rationale is based on risk avoidance or reduction, with an eye on the capital needs. This policy is of a microprudential nature, as no explicit references to financial stability or systemic considerations have been included in the directive's provisions. But some of the relevant provisions of the directive are indirectly based on financial stability concerns that may be triggered by excessive risk taking, itself induced by too strong incentives.

The remuneration regime is applicable to all individual banks, large or not, their parent company and the bank's subsidiaries, wherever located. The rule has a clear extraterritorial ambit: the rule would be applicable to banks, which are located in the Union but are subsidiaries of non-EU groups. It would also apply to subsidiaries of EU banks located outside the Union, whether for the calculation of remuneration on a group basis, or for the subsidiary individually. The broad ambit avoids the rule to be evaded. The directive's formulation excludes subsidiaries of the same parent that are not subsidiaries of the bank – i.e. sister companies and their group entities – what might be of importance for bank-insurance groups. The restrictions do not apply to the insurance part of the group, not as an insurance company, nor as a company owned by the same parent as the bank.

The directive rules are applicable to executives, but also to non-executives[58], not only to directors, but also to material risk takers. Again, independent directors are not mentioned but they should normally not receive a bonus, as this would affect their independence[59]. 'Risk takers', i.e. staff members that are in a position that is directly responsible for, or linked to the risk activity of the bank have been reported to receiving very high bonuses which have been linked to the results of their aggressive activity leading to considerable risk for the bank. The definition of risk takers has been further detailed in a Commission delegated regulation,

---

[57] A referendum was held in Switzerland aimed at limiting remuneration in listed c companies to 12 times the average lowest paid remuneration. It was defeated on 24 November 2014 www.swissinfo.ch/eng/salary-cap-fails-at-ballot-box/37362410. See for details about remunerations in Swiss listed companies: ETHOS, "Verguetungen 2013 fuer fuehrende Instanzen 100 groesste in der Schweiz kotierte Unternehmen", www.ethosfund.ch/upload/publication/p530d_141008_Vergtungen_der_Fhrungsinstanzen_der_grssten_in_der_Schweiz_kotierten_Unternehmen_Kurzfassung_.pdf (2014).

[58] See for the position and remuneration of non-executives directors, HAY GROUP, "Non-executive directors in Europe, 2013 Casting light on pay practices, structures and diversity of leading European companies", www.haygroup.com/be/press/details.aspx?id=43106.

[59] The independence of directors is not a great help, rather should directors be more expert, according to M. Becht, P. Bolton and A. Roell, nt. 1.

qualifying these risk takers as 'identified persons'[60]. Their number is often quite considerable, leading to wide-spread risk awareness in the bank.

The directive's regime is based on the distinction between fixed and variable remuneration. Both terms have been defined in article 91(1), leaving no room for a third form of remuneration. 'Fixed' is that part of the remuneration that 'primarily'[61] reflects "the relevant professional experience and organisational responsibility" of the employee. It is part of the job description of the employee as formulated in his terms of employment. 'Variable remuneration' reflects the performance of the employee on the basis of sustainable and risk-adjusted performance, including performance in excess of that. Three levels of performance can be taken into account: that of the bank in general, the profits of the department where the beneficiary is employed and finally his individual contribution. This type of remuneration is usually referred to as 'bonuses'. Both definitions are followed by the European Banking Authority to analyse the nature of a remuneration: on that basis the 'allowances' were qualified as variable remuneration[62]. How risk and performance have to be linked has been analysed by the BCBS[63].

There are no express restrictions applicable to the fixed remuneration but it would be subject to supervisory review on the basis of the general criteria for the remuneration policy such as "professional experience and organisational responsibility"[64], but also taking into account the bank's "size, internal organisation and nature, scope and complexity of activities"[65]. It would seem that supervisors would not intervene in this largely discretionary matter, except in very 'extraordinary, outrageous' cases. It is important to conclude that banks remain largely free in determining the fixed part of the remuneration the more so as the fixed part serves as the calculation basis for the variable part. This approach implies that the directive would not allow a remuneration that would

---

[60]   Commission delegated regulation (EU) No. 604/2014 of 4 March 2014 supplementing Directive 2013/36/EU of the European Parliament and of the Council with regard to regulatory technical standards with respect to qualitative and appropriate quantitative criteria to identify categories of staff whose professional activities have a material impact on an institution's risk profile, OJ.EU 6 June 2014.

[61]   The meaning of this addition probably refers to the fact that the remuneration may be related to other elements.

[62]   See about the 'allowances': EBA Opinion, 15 October 2014, EBA/Op/2014/10: EBA "is of the view that 'role-based allowances' which are not predetermined, are not transparent to staff, are not permanent, provide incentives to take risks or, without prejudice to national law, are revocable, should not be considered as fixed remuneration but should be classified as variable in line with the letter and purpose of the CRD. The amount paid is not fixed, is not permanent, i.e. maintained over time for the specific role and organisational responsibilities, can be understood as being indirectly performance-related given that its review depends on cost and benefit considerations, is neither set out in a pre-defined objective manner nor is transparent to staff and therefore does not promote sound and effective risk management, and is based on other contractual conditions which do not form part of routine employment packages". The reaction of the Bank of England was sharp: Speech by Andrew Bailey, Director PRA, 16 October 2014 "the bonus cap is the wrong policy, the debate around it is misguided, and the best thing I can say about allowances is that they are a response to a bad policy."

[63]   Basel Committee on Banking Supervision: Range of Methodologies for Risk and Performance Alignment of Remuneration, May 2011.

[64]   On the basis of art. 92 (1) stating that the supervisors will ensure application of this part of the Directive.

[65]   Art. 92(2) first §, CRD IV.

only consist of a variable amount, or, as is usual in the US, that the fixed part is a minimal amount while the effective amount is mainly represented by the variable part, that is than very considerable indeed.

EBA collects and publishes data on remuneration of high earners: an update version with date adapted to CRD IV is expected[66].

The variable part is limited, according to the directive, to 100% of the fixed part. If it would be more, the general meeting of shareholders has to give its approval, but it should never exceed 200% of the fixed part. The role of the AGM is to approve the higher maximum ratio, not to approve the remuneration itself. The directive's approach is different from the 'say on pay' formula that has received wide attention and seems to have contributed to a fall in overall remuneration[67]. From the 2012 figures published for 'high earners' it would seem that a ceiling of 100% would allow many of them to keep the same bonus, while 200% would allow continuity for a very large part, except in investment banking and to a lesser extent asset management[68].

Apart from these quantitative limits, the directive imposes a further series of restrictions applicable to the variable remuneration. Many of these already belonged to standard practise. These can only be listed here:
–   variable remuneration should be based on individual and collective performance, including non-financial criteria;
–   set on a multi-year basis for measuring performance;
–   payments are to be deferred, and spread over the business cycle, including the related present and future risks;
–   payments should not endanger the capital basis or its later build up;
–   it should be consistent with sound risk management;
–   guaranteed variable remuneration is only exceptionally allowed, as relating to new staff for their first year[69];
–   balance between fix and variable: fixed should allow flexible variable policy, possibly even excluding variable[70];
–   ratio of fixed and variable, as explained above;

---

[66]   Art. 75 of Directive 2013/36/EC (CRDIV); see also: EBA, The guidelines for the data collection can be found at www.eba.europa.eu/regulation-andpolicy/remuneration/guidelines-on-the-data-collection-exercise-regarding-high-earners   and   www.eba.europa.eu/documents/10180/111703/EBA-GL-2012-04---GL-4-on-remuneration-benchmarking-exercise-.pdf; BCBS, Pillar 3 disclosure requirements for remuneration, July 2011.
[67]   See R.S. THOMAS and Chr. VAN DER ELST, "The international Scope of Say on Pay", September 2013, ECGI, *Law Working Paper*, 227/2013 analysing the factors that lead to effectiveness of say on pay; for the US: R.S. RANDALL, A.R. PALMITER and J.F. COTTER, "Dodd-Frank's Say on Pay; Will it lead to a Greater role for shareholders in corporate governance?" 97 Cornell L.R. (2012), http://cornell.lawreviewnetwork.com/files/2013/02/Thomas-et-al-final2.pdf; see further "The Swiss regulation", Verordnung gegen übermässige Vergütungen bei börsenkotierten Aktiengesellschaften, (VegüV), 20 November 2013, www.admin.ch/opc/de/classified-compilation/20132519/index.html, and the analysis by Ethos, nt. 57.
[68]   EBA, High Earners 2012 Data, figure 14-17.
[69]   See art. 94 (1)(d) and (e), only allowed for new employment and for their first year.
[70]   94 (1)(f),CRD IV.

- discount rate for future payments: on 25% of variable for five year deferred instruments[71];
- special situation variable payments: early termination payments (golden parachutes) reflect time in office, 'golden welcomes' reflect long term interest of the bank;
- payment in risk bearing instruments for at least 50% of the variable remuneration; these have been defined in a Regulation[72]; a retention policy will apply;
- payment or vesting deferral for at least 40%;
- clawbacks and malus rules;
- pension payment deferral policy for early leavers;
- no hedging or similar techniques annulling the retention or deferral rules allowed;
- no evasion of Directive or CRR.

The most difficult issue relates to the practical consequences of these new provisions: what has been or will be the effect of these and similar measures? As in several EU Member States the new rules will only be applicable from 2014 on, the available information is limited to trends over the previous periods. The comparison is made more difficult as the way the Member states have implemented the directive – or are still in the process of doing so – is quite different, some imposing a stricter cap, others introducing additional provisions[73].

In terms of findings the following trends can already be observed:

The level of fixed remuneration has increased while the variable part has been decreased. This finding has been made by several authors and is evident from too angles: first banks are reluctant to reduce the level of total remuneration out of fear of loosing their best staff; secondly, if the total amount is to be maintained, only by increasing the fixed part can the objective be secured. Capping the variable part leads to an increase in the fixed part, with the objective of attaining the maximum amount in the variable part. The net result has been an increase of total, and especially of fixed remuneration.

According to the EBA, using pre CRD IV data, where the total amount of the remuneration paid to 'identified staff', calculated per staff member, has decreased

---

[71] For details about the discount rate, see: EBA, *Guidelines on the applicable notional discount rate for variable remuneration*, 27 March 2014, EBA/GL/2014/ 01.

[72] Commission delegated regulation (EU) 527/2014 of 12 March 2014 supplementing directive 2013/36... with regard to regulatory technical standards specifying the classes of instruments that adequately reflect the credit quality of an institution as a going concern and are appropriate to be used for the purposes of variable remuneration, *O.J.L.* 148/21, 20 May 2014.

[73] As has been allowed by the directive, the Belgian cap is 50% as is the Danish cap while the Dutch cap will be 20%. Have adopted the directive's restrictions: France, the UK, Germany.

somewhat from 2010 to 2012, the variable part has decreased twice (30%) as much as the increase of the fixed part (31%). This corresponds to a fall in the ratio Variable/Fixed from 204,76% to 108,74% for each 'indentified staff member'. Per business line the decrease of the ratio was the largest for investment banking followed by asset management, and much lower for retail banking[74].

A different trend is found in a 2014 report by McLagan[75], dealing with a somewhat different population (bank and capital market professionals mainly from investment banks) pointing to a fall in overall remuneration between 2009 and 2013 from 100 to 77%%, or even 65% for the EMEA area. Individual compensation per head fell less, 12% and 20% respectively. The bonus pool was almost halved leading to an individual fall in bonuses to 66% and 62%. Fixed pay has increased considerably, from 30% of total compensation to 62%, stable for about three years while variable dropped from 70% to 38% of total compensation. These differences between the EBA and the McLagan survey are probably due to differences in the population, as EBA data covers the entire banking sector. While in the McLagan data, only part of the investment bank staff was analysed.

This downward trend is only partially due to regulation; according to the consultancy firm Tower Watson[76], only11% (UK, v 21 in Germany) can be attributed to regulatory and political pressures, while 84% (v 63% in Germany) to business, economic and competitive presses. Recent data indicate that banks have adapted their remuneration policies, in order to retain staff.

Variable remuneration has a significant impact on risk taking at the level of traders. This finding has been illustrated in a paper by Efing, Hau, Kampkoeter and Steinbrecher[77] finding a robust correlation of pay incentives and the bank's trading income, concluding that "large bonus payments seem to have incentivised risk-taking that was excessive from the perspective of the NPV maximisation". Whether that would apply to the members of the board of directors is debatable as board are less involved in individual risk taking, unless with respect to decisions that directly affect the risk profile (e.g. an intended acquisition, or a specific strategy).

The comparison with the US pay practices is difficult to make as in US banks it is traditional to pay a small percentage of overall pay in fixed remuneration (5 to 14% for a sample of the largest banks), leading to a high ratio for variable

---

[74] See also TOWERS WATSON, *The impact of European Regulation on Pay in Financial services*, Figure 03., May 2012.
[75] MCLAGAN, "Review of the Reward Environment in the Banking Industry, Association Financial Markets Europe", January 2015 www.afme.eu/searchresults.aspx?searchText=McLagan&FolderID=0&Recursive= true&SearchFor=all&OrderBy=rank&ResultsPageSize=10.
[76] TOWERS WATSON, Table 04.
[77] EFING, HAU, KAMPKOETER and STEINBRECHER, nt 70.

remuneration. Here the total amount of remuneration will give a better view: in the US, for most investment banks, the total amounted to 15 to 20 m $. The total nominal amount for EU banks varied between 1m euro to 6 up to 10 m. euro, the French, Italian and Nordic banks being in the lowest range. As to the ratio in the EU, continental CEO's ratio was between 0,4 and 1,9 variable v fixed, with considerably higher ratios for the UK and for the largest German bank.

Total remuneration remaining equal, would more fixed remuneration be preferable over variable? In terms of incentives for risk taking, a higher variable part is logically an incentive for higher risk taking, at least of expected higher returns on investment. By increasing the fixed part, one could state that staff will be less sensitive to the returns they achieve making the bank more vulnerable to business cycles and downturns. The cap on bonuses would incite staff to take risk up to he level of the bonus, but not beyond letting some better deals aside, or as it is presented, to take the bad risk and let aside the good ones[78]. As variable pay is linked to performance, by reducing it, performance will suffer but will not reduce the overall pay package.

Some further effects are also mentioned in the discussion about remuneration. Lower remuneration would lead valuable staff to leaving the firm for activities in other less regulated sectors, or even for emigrating abroad. Hiring of new top performers would become more difficult, leading to loss of competitiveness of the industry concerned. This argument was also frequently heard when the hedge fund regulation AIFMD was introduced in the EU. Some related the increase in fixed salary to this factor, leading to "issues with sound business management"[79]. As the fixed part in the total salary package will increase, inflexibility will result, leading to reductions in employment to manage the total pay package. As the impact of incentives is reduced, strong performance management will be affected.

Several types of remuneration competition should be distinguished: apart from competition with less regulated jurisdictions, there is competition with other economic sectors and with other types of employment[80]. Inter-sectoral competition is known in the economy in general. Other factors than remuneration are important: the difference between gross and net remuneration also plays a role, such as the drastic increase of the tax rate to 75% which frightened foreign executives to be active in France, although it is reported to have little impact on French residents.

---

[78]   K. MURPHY, *Regulating Banking Bonuses in the European Union: A case study in Unintended Consequences*, April 2013, ssrn No. 2235395.
[79]   TOWERS WATSON, nt 61, p. 6.
[80]   TOWERS WATSON, nt. 61, p. 6, mentioning that pay levels for accounting or finance entry positions was lower than in other UK industries.

In the financial sector, there is competition with other financial activities such as asset management or insurance, The CRDIV treats asset managers if organised as investment firms are subject to the same regime as banks, both being called 'institutions'. In the asset management field, Specific regulation has been adopted dealing with the remuneration for UCITS[81] managers and managers of alternative investment funds (AIFMD)[82]. In each of these cases however there are no mandatory ratios between fixed and variable remuneration. In the insurance field, there are no comparable restrictions. But an in house entity may qualify as an asset manager. National remuneration rules should however also be taken into account. Moreover listed companies are subject to their own governance and remuneration rules, mostly consisting of giving shareholders a 'say on pay'.

Difficult to measure would be the effects of the regulation on changes in the legal capacity in which the services are rendered, such as employees offering their services in company name, or as independent experts.

9.9. CONCLUSION

Corporate governance of banks has become a topic on its own, increasingly distant from general governance thinking. It is serving as a source of inspiration for similar developments in other sectors, especially for listed companies. Especially the remuneration debate has become a rich source of analysis and controversy that is not likely to be settled very soon, at the same time giving rise to attractive consultancy. Although the risk profile of banks seem to have decreased, whether this can be attributed to changes in the governance rules is open for debate: so may other factors have contributed to raising awareness and reducing remuneration that only over time will one be able to establish a credible relationship between governance and the recovered health of the banking system.

---

[81] Ucits 5 directive, nt 11.
[82] See nt. 13.

50 YEARS OF MONEY AND FINANCE – LESSONS AND CHALLENGES

SUERF commemorates its 50th anniversary with a special volume entitled "50 Years of Money and Finance: Lessons and Challenges", published by Larcier. The researchers who have contributed to the volume were asked to look at the monetary and financial history of the last 50 years, and to summarise the most important trends and experiences and to then draw conclusions for the future. They were asked to identify the main trends in international financial markets, in global and European macroeconomic (im)balances, in European financial integration, in central banking, in banking and securities markets, in financial innovation and in the origins and handling of financial crises. Path-breaking events, politicial decisions and relevant outstanding research contributions in the field since the early 1960s all feature significantly. Edited by Morten Balling and Ernest Gnan, with a foreword by Christian Noyer, preface by Urs Birchler and an introduction by the editors, and concluding with a timeline of the major events of the last fifty years, the book consists of the following chapters:

- Global and European Monetary Arrangements: from Bretton Woods to EMU
  Niels THYGESEN

- Global and Euro Imbalances: China and Germany
  Guonan MA and Robert N. MCCAULEY

- Is Monetary Policy a Science? The Interaction of Theory and Practice over the Last 50 Years
  William R. WHITE

- Unconventional Monetary Policy of the ECB during the Financial Crisis: an Assessment and New Evidence
  Christiaan PATTIPEILOHY, Jan Willem VAN DEN END, Mostafa TABBAE, Jon FROST and Jakob DE HAAN

- The development of financial markets and financial theory: 50 years of interaction
  Morten BALLING and Ernest GNAN

- Integration versus Interdependence and Complexity in Global Trade and Finance in the Post-War Period
  Paul ATKINSON, Adrian BLUNDELL-WIGNALL and Caroline ROULET

- From National towards European/Global Financial Regulation
  Charles A.E. GOODHART

- The Evolution of Financial Supervision: the Continuing Search for the Holy Grail
  Donato MASCIANDARO and Marc QUINTYN

- Fifty Years in the Evolution of Bank Business Models
  David T. LLEWELLYN

- Performance in European Banking: Productivity, Profitability and Employment Trends
  Philip MOLYNEUX

- Shadow Banking and New Lending Channels – Past and Future
  Patricia JACKSON

- The 2007- Financial Crisis – a EURO-pean Perspective
  Juan AYUSO and Roberto BLANCO

- The Effects of Derivatives on Underlying Financial Markets: Equity Options, Commodity Derivatives and Credit Default Swaps
  William ARRATA, Alejandro BERNALES and Virginie COUDERT

www.suerf.org/50yearsofmoneyandfinance

SUERF – Société Universitaire Européenne de Recherches Financières

SUERF is incorporated in France as a non-profit-making Association. It was founded in 1963 as a European-wide forum with the aim of bringing together professionals from both the practitioner and academic sides of finance who have an interest in the working of financial markets, institutions and systems, and the conduct of monetary and regulatory policy. SUERF is a network association of central bankers, bankers and other practitioners in the financial sector, and academics with the purpose of analysing and understanding European financial markets, institutions and systems, and the conduct of regulation and monetary policy. It organises regular Colloquia, lectures and seminars and each year publishes several analytical studies in the form of *SUERF Studies*.

SUERF has its full-time permanent Executive Office and Secretariat located at the Austrian National Bank in Vienna. It is financed by annual corporate, personal and academic institution membership fees. Corporate membership currently includes major European financial institutions and Central Banks. SUERF is strongly supported by Central Banks in Europe and its membership comprises most of Europe's Central Banks (including the Bank for International Settlements and the European Central Bank), banks, other financial institutions and academics.

SUERF Studies

1997-2012

For details of *SUERF Studies* published prior to 2013 (Nos. 1 to 22 and 2003/1-2012/5) please consult the SUERF website at www.suerf.org/suerfstudies.

2013

2013/1   *The Interaction of Political, Fiscal and Financial Stability: Lessons from the Crisis*, edited by Ernest Gnan, Vienna 2013, ISBN 978-3-902109-66-8

2013/2   *States, Banks and the Financing of the Economy: Fiscal Policy and Sovereign Risk Perspectives*, edited by Morten Balling, Peter Egger and Ernest Gnan, Vienna 2013, ISBN 978-3-902109-67-5

| 2013/3 | *States, Bankings and the Financing of the Economy: Monetary Policy and Regualtory Perspectives*, edited by Morten Balling, Ernest Gnan and Patricia Jackson, Vienna 2013, ISBN 978-3-902109-68-2 |

| 2013/4 | *Property Prices and Real Estate Financing in a Turbulent World*, edited by Morten Balling and Jesper Berg, Vienna 2013, ISBN 978-3-902109-70-5 |

| 2013/5 | *The Future of Sovereign Borrowing in Europe*, edited by Morten Balling, Ernest Gnan and Johannes Holler, Vienna 2013, ISBN 978-3-902109-71-2 |

2014

| 2014/1 | *The Effectiveness of Capital Adequacy Measures in Predicting Bank Distress*, by David G. Mayes and Hanno Stremmel, Vienna 2014, ISBN 978-3-902109-72-9 |

| 2014/2 | *The Value of Banks and Their Business Models to Society*, edited by Jakob de Haan and Allard Bruinshoofd, Vienna 2014, ISBN 978-3-902109-73-6 |

| 2014/3 | *Banking after regulatory reforms – business as usual?*, edited by Esa Jokivuolle and Jouko Vilmunen, Vienna 2014, ISBN 978-3-902109-74-3 |

| 2014/4 | *Money, Regulation & Growth: financing new growth in Europe*, edited by and introduction by Marc Quintyn, Donato Masciandaro, Frank Lierman and Morten Balling, Vienna, 2014, ISBN: 978-3-902109-75-0 |